Testimonials for

"Bridges to Success: How to Transform Learning Difficulties".

*"**Bridges to Success** provides refreshing and empowering tools for adults who know children with learning difficulties. Olive backs up these strategies with explanations and anecdotes from people she has helped, as well as her own experiences. She demonstrates supreme skill by being able to break down seemingly complex problems into a series of simple, easy to resolve challenges, and offers replicable strategies that can be tried by anyone in a position to help these children – parents, carers, teachers and childminders, to name a few. Her passion comes across powerfully and this book reflects her generosity. Olive wants people to know about how simple this can be. She is prepared to ask some challenging questions, make some fascinating observations...and offer answers. What could happen if we were all to employ a child-centred approach to at least one young person we know? As Olive says "When you know something works, you have to offer it to others." I for one am very grateful to have seen my own children transform – and as a parent, that is just about the best reward possible."* **Karen Moxom, CEO of the Association for NLP (and mother of two boys)**

"A refreshing, practical and powerful book drawing on Olive's own extensive experience in the field of education, and her work with children and families, including those with learning difficulties. She has incorporated concepts from Energetic NLP throughout, including very useful descriptions of visualisations, and other techniques that can easily be used with children and their families. Powerful and inspiring real life case studies are used to illustrate key points, showing the dramatic impact of using the skills described in practice. This book will be an eye-opener for families and for anyone working with young people in the fields of education and healthcare." **Dr Arti Maini MBBS BSc (Hons) MSc Med Ed, MRCGP, GP, Coach, Medical Educationalist and NLP Master Practitioner**

"This book provides an uplifting, positive and innovative way to approaching learning. Olive has combined her passion, her life experiences alongside her practitioner experiences to bring to life holistic and refreshing techniques, to not only help support children with difficulties but also to incorporate strategies that the family and surrounding caregivers can also try. The strengths of the book are precisely that, children with learning difficulties should not be seen as having a deficit

but that they have great strengths and ability. Learning techniques should therefore be adapted to account for this unique strength that these children possess. This book gets away from "fix what the individual" focusing on fostering what is best within these children by using new techniques to help utilise their strengths. It presents a refreshing and exciting change to approaching learning difficulties; people should listen and take note." **Dr Keely Gunson, Researcher in Health Psychology, University of Bath.**

"Olive's practical approach to learning is both simple and engaging. Her case work and her personal experience of learning difficulties help her bring a rich perspective to these issues which focus on how students can easily improve their learning skills. My undergraduate computing students really benefited from her different approach, using visualisation to learn new programming techniques." **Dr. Herbert Daly, Lecturer, University of Bedfordshire, UK**

"This is a phenomenal book which has some amazing contents! It offers a wide ranging menu of exciting, if not different, options which draw upon Olive's background knowledge and experience when working with young people and adults with Specific Learning Difficulties (SpLD). At its heart, visualisation is the key and much Neuro-linguistic Programming (NLP) is brought into play. This combination is used to investigate, stimulate and change individual needs in a variety of ways. For those engaged in education, if offers a new approach to the teaching of many essential life skills, inclusive of reading and spelling. However, of greater importance is the overview of the individual which allows social and emotional aspects and experiences to be included as well. The book itself was originally compiled for the SpLD population but, in my opinion, would also prove of value to help anyone with other examples of special educational needs (SEN). As a teacher of over thirty years experience, many of these associated with SEN students of all types and abilities, I would have liked access to this resource many years ago! It's an easy book to read. It provides examples of case study experiences from all walks of life and is written with the personal touch. So, whether teacher, social worker, trainer or coach, it will engage you as soon as you open to the first page. I wholeheartedly recommend it to you!" **Brian J. Sparks, MA(Ed) MEd BEd (Hons) PGDip (Education) SpLD AMBDA SpLD APC (Patoss) NPQH AdvDipEd (Open) Adv Cert Ed. Former Special Needs Coordinator [mainstream Secondary School] and now Specialist Dyslexia Teacher. Vice Chair of the Somerset Dyslexia Association.**

Bridges to Success:

How to Transform Learning Difficulties

Simple skills for families and teachers to bring success to those with
SpLD – Dyslexia, Dyscalculia, ADHD, Dyspraxia, Tourette's Syndrome,
Asperger's Syndrome or Autism using NLP and Energetic NLP

By
OLIVE HICKMOTT

www.bridgestosuccess.co.uk

Published by
MX Publishing
A New Perspectives Book

For more information about the book take a look at:
www.bridgestosuccess.co.uk and the author's associated practice
www.empoweringlearning.co.uk

ISBN Paperback 9781908218780
ISBN ePub 9781908218797
ISBN PDF 9781908218803

First published in 2011
© Copyright 2011
Olive Hickmott

Although every effort has been made to ensure the accuracy of the information contained in this guide as of the date of publication, nothing herein should be construed as giving specific treatment advice. In addition, the application of the techniques to specific circumstances can present complex issues that are beyond the scope of this guide. This publication is intended to provide general information pertaining to developing these skills.

Published in the UK by MX Publishing, 335, Princess Park Manor, Royal Drive, London, N11 3GX

www.mxpublishing.co.uk

Dedication

I would like to dedicate this book to all those individuals and families who have given freely of their own experiences with learning difficulties, so that they can help others.

"THIS BOOK WILL CHANGE YOUR VIEW OF LEARNING
DIFFICULTIES"

In the words of Labi Siffre:
"Something inside me so strong,
I know that I can make it
You thought that my pride was gone
Oh no, something inside so strong"

Others resources for Learning Difficulties:

Previous New Perspectives books:
Seeing Spells Achieving

New Perspectives CDs:
Pass Literacy On
Waldorf – the dog who isn't word-blind
A talking book for "Bridges to Success"
The meditations in "Bridges to Success"

All available from www.empoweringlearning.co.uk

About the Author

My name is Olive Hickmott. My passion is helping those with chronic/acute illness and/or learning difficulties set, achieve and surpass their goals. I'm lucky enough to be doing what I consider the best job in the world. I'm an inveterate puzzle-solver. These challenges and their causes can be the greatest puzzles of all for an individual to unravel. Luckily, the clues and keys lie within us. We have such fabulous self-healing skills; it's just a question of learning how to access them.

I am a NLP Master Practitioner, Accredited Energetic NLP Practitioner, a Thought Pattern Management Master Practitioner and a Certified Coach. Utilising my training I work with individuals and groups, enabling personal growth in all aspects of their lives. It's a great privilege to be there at the moment when an individual first grasps the interlinking of mind, body and spirit, and gets their first glimpse of what they can achieve.

I also work within businesses to improve the well-being of both staff and directors, improving their communication and relationships and ultimately the profitability that results from a smoother running organisation. I left my own corporate life as an Engineering Director in 1990 and founded my own business. I am a Director of the Hickmott Partnership and The International Association for Health and Learning.

I have become an expert in how people learn visually and how they can make the best use of their visual skills. Creative visual learning is an exceptional skill that is currently under-acknowledged. ©Empowering Learning is the name I use in coaching individuals and families, to understand and in many instances overcome the symptoms and causes of learning difficulties. I also teach programmes to educationalists worldwide.

I focus on primary research working with those people who recognise their specific challenges. They have helped me develop and articulate the self empowered *New Perspectives* approach to well-being. Without their valuable assistance, this would not have been possible.

Additional Assistance

If you need any additional help with any part of this book, please contact me, Olive Hickmott, via olive@empoweringlearning.co.uk

This book and associated CDs, downloads etc. has its own web site www.bridgestosuccess.co.uk. You will find additional resources there; such as a talking book (for those who find reading a challenge or are short of time), a CD of all the guided imagery meditations from the book and the Waldorf stories for very young children. Everyone who buys this book is entitled to download a free workbook and visual self-assessment. I'm also asking readers to let me have feedback on their experiences so this can help others and provide additional tools.

Of course there are benefits from working with an experienced coach. I would be delighted to offer you any further assistance you may need. We always answer requests for assistance, throughout the world. There is a growing network of international individuals, who are able to offer local coaching and training. If you are suitably experienced or want to be trained please just mail me and apply to join the group.

Please follow me on:

Blog: www.olivehickmott.wordpress.com
Twitter: www.twitter.com/olivehickmott
LinkedIn: www.linkedin.com/in/olivehickmott
Facebook: www.facebook.com/olive.hickmott

Acknowledgements

There are many people I wish to thank for their help and influence in writing this book:

Especially Art Giser, creator of Energetic NLP, (www.energeticNLP.com) Ian McDermott, Robert Dilts, Tim Hallbom, Suzi Smith and Peter King for their invaluable training programmes.

Caroline Chapple, for her fabulous illustrations; she has the great skill to be able to bring my ideas to life on the page. www.chapplecoaching.com

All those colleagues who have given me feedback on the book. I should like to especially thank Jan Doole and Brian Sparks for their invaluable contributions to the final draft.

Finally, my family who not only read parts of the draft, have challenged my thinking and above all supported me throughout the project. In particular, my son, Alec Fazackerley Hickmott, who has, with his skills for succinct clarity, made an exceptional contribution as my editor and writing mentor.

I am indebted to those I meet, whose names have been changed in this book, for providing such valuable information about their own experiences. They are always pleased to be helping others in this way.

Contents

Index of simple skills:

Preface – a Personal Note

There are few greater pleasures in the world than to see a young person's face light up as they change their experience with, for example, reading, spelling, numeracy, confidence, organising their thoughts and feeling better about themselves. Their smiles are quite infectious.

This is my experience on a daily basis; I want to share it with you to help young people start transforming their learning difficulties. In my experience many people do learn differently, needing encouragement and a little training to put their exceptional skills to best use.

By today's standards I would have been diagnosed with Dyslexia as a child, due to my dreadful spelling and hatred of reading. When my turn came to be asked to read aloud I wanted to sink through the floor, in embarrassment. I never read a book for pleasure until around the age of forty and it was very difficult to recall what I had read. Most of my life my brain has been hyperactive and my behaviour sometimes quite like ADHD, even to the point of being unsteady on my feet and showing dyspraxic tendencies. A teacher once told my mother that my brain was far too fast for my hand. This was nearly accurate. As a result of doing this work, I have retained my ability to see different perspectives and "let go" of my crippling confusion over spelling and reading.

I realise that I have a very different perspective on many things, and I have written this book to share these different approaches that I have used, to help others.

When I first discovered that good spellers could see words in their head, I was dumfounded that I had never even thought of trying this. I was then furious that no-one had told me about this skill, which others had taken for granted. I quickly turned this into a passion to offer these skills to others. Then I discovered there were other, equally important, skills that could change peoples' experience of learning, and I wanted to pass on these key messages to others with learning difficulties.

In my experience many of the symptoms categorised today as SpLDs are actually behaviours learnt in response to learning differences, which a young person does not understand. These behaviours become a habit, with the young person assuming that their experience is the same as that of others, whereas theirs is often very different.

Once you understand your own experiences better and learn some simple ways to do things differently, it becomes so much easier to change these unhelpful habits.

The challenge is how to get these valuable skills out to the "man/woman in the street". I am passionate about people learning new skills and passing them on to their friends, family, educationalists and work colleagues.

> I recall a day teaching a number of children visual spelling in Primary School. As I passed through the playground at lunchtime there was one of the six year olds teaching her friends who had not been in the class. What a delight!

To achieve this, collaboration at all levels is essential. This book contains references to other peoples' work. A generative collaboration, where the result is more than the individual parts, is the key to achieving this change for future generations and a vehicle for supporting research into the areas covered in this book. To create change in any system you need a mixture of practical experience, research, influence and motivation. Our children are the essential motivation and in the words of Dr. Randolph Blackwell, "We are trying to make it impossible for anyone to argue that it can't be done, by demonstrating what can be done."

I see young people as having exceptional skills. At the same time the challenge is **how to** "help" them achieve their goals. This book will help you see the world from their perspective and understand their skills.

I have no formal educational and medical training. My observations and experience have enabled me to develop techniques that complement conventional approaches, empowering the individual to take action, using resources they already possess, to positively affect their health and any learning challenges.

This book includes Neuro-linguistic Programming (NLP) and Energetic NLP[1] processes; you will learn here all the information you need. Energetic NLP is a unique blend of NLP, intuition development and energetic healing.

I was the child who always asked "why should we do ....?" and "how does that work?" I have learnt so much from clients, understanding more and more about how each individual brain wants and needs to work, to find learning easier. I don't pretend to know all the answers for every learning difficulty as I am continually learning, but the understanding you will gain from this book will give you many new perspectives to try.

In *Seeing Spells Achieving*[2] I talked about a particular client, Frank. A teacher had said of him. "He won't remember what you've said. He has a brain tumour. It moves and he forgets everything he's learnt." Astonished at the comment and the concept, I taught him to improve his literacy through visual memory, with excellent results – he never forgot what I taught him, and the comment about the brain tumour seemed to have little or no relevance to his ability with literacy. If I had bought into what I had been told, I would have been stuck too.

I am always encouraged by the words of Ralph Waldo Emerson, "Whatever course you decide upon, there is always someone to tell you that you are wrong. There are always difficulties arising which tempt you to believe that your critics are right. To map out a course of action and follow it to an end requires courage."

My dream is to be able to couple my ability to see different perspectives with my infectious enthusiasm, for believing anything is possible if we just know how to do it, to enable people to transform learning difficulties and shine.

Like my clients, I want readers of this book to say, "That makes sense", "I feel like a kid with a new toy!" We all have the answers inside ourselves, and benefit from some clear signposts.

Olive Hickmott, 2011

Introduction

How We Learn

The ability to successfully learn new skills is fundamental to the existence of every living creature. As we grow up we continually acquire new skills naturally, often with little education. For some people, however, their natural capabilities pull them in another direction and conventional learning is much harder. When children don't naturally acquire the required skills, the world becomes more confusing and they may often become identified as being "learning disabled."

In recent years more and more learning difficulties have been identified as Specific Learning Difficulties (SpLD). Such diagnoses or "labels," as many people refer to them, have both good and bad aspects. In many respects, such labels serve as shorthand for the range of challenges a young person is facing, helping people understand more about their condition and to provide them with extra support. The downside is that labels can keep people very stuck in their condition, contributing to a feeling of disempowerment that prevents young people, their parents and teachers from trying to change their situation. Adding to the confusion, there is often much variation, even within an SpLD with young people exhibiting just a few or many of the symptoms. In addition not all learning difficulties are diagnosed, for a variety of reasons.

It is possible to move beyond such a confusing and seemingly intractable situation. As I have seen throughout my professional experience, people with SpLD often have exceptional skills that allow them to see things differently, and to be creative in ways that we may not even comprehend. Indeed, their exceptional skills can dramatically support and sometimes completely transform the debilitating symptoms. Though confusion is often the downside of such exceptional skills, this book will show that the skills don't have to *cause* the confusion, but can in fact be employed to remedy a whole variety of unfortunate symptoms.

Throughout the wide spectrum of SpLD, I see a common pattern of exceptional people manifesting often quite debilitating confusion. As you learn more, you will realise the connections between these two polarised views of an individual. I can see past the problems to the exceptional skills and gifts these people have, considering how these skills are affecting other aspects of their life.

Understanding Their Experience

Increasingly, people are realising that these young people and adults learn differently but don't know how to ensure that the skills they are using work effectively. For example, someone might learn visually, with their pictures flying around so fast they can't keep them still. This "difficulty" could be used as a fabulous creative skill for making

up stories, animation or graphic design for example, but would be a poor strategy for remembering

how to spell words. In such cases, young people can learn an additional skill to help them regain control of their visual memory, allowing them to focus on still pictures. Unfortunately, if no one notices a young person is using the wrong strategy, it can result in mounting confusion for them as they get older.

Working with a huge range of clients over the last seven years, aged from four to eighty-five years old, I have been privileged to gain insights into how confusion develops and deepens with time. For example, what starts off as simple letter reversals (a four year old not knowing the difference between p, q, b and d) can develop into them seeing whole words moving on the page, then whole pages moving and eventually to a hatred of reading. Accompanying this development, the young person's behaviour will often deteriorate. They may then not want to go to school, undoubtedly contributing to the many disaffected young people we see today. Is this really surprising when opening a book generates so much confusion for the young person, often accompanied by a physical feeling of nausea?

It follows that any improvement in the prevention of SpLDs is so important to prevent the start of this spiral of confusion. A few teachers are already integrating these new skills, presented here, into their classroom curriculum. It only takes minutes to teach these to four year olds, reducing or preventing confusion from the very start.

I know change is needed in education when you have a perfectly articulate twenty-five year old, who is brave enough to confront his fears, say that all he wants is "to be able to read a menu when he takes his girlfriend out for a meal". Rather than focusing on deficits, this book shows how education, based on a deeper understanding of how people learn, can help young people learn the skills that others pick up naturally and subconsciously. As I will show, the most valid approach is for us to learn where their confusion is coming from, and then teach young people skills so they can learn **how to** change their experience.

Most approaches to SpLDs focus on the individual having a variety of deficits and limitations. As such, educators often "over teach" the same techniques without any awareness of the possibility that they have the wrong strategy in place. By contrast, my child-centred approach attempts to see the world and the learning process from the young person's perspective. I identify the positive skills "learning disabled" children possess, helping them to employ these skills in other aspects of their lives. The invaluable addition is to look at how people without SpLDs learn successfully, and integrate their strategies into the **how to** skills to teach others, to overcome their symptoms.

These form the basis of this book, enabling parents and teachers to help children learn more effectively by introducing some invaluable **how to** skills. The negative emotions and the frequent frustration that surround those with SpLDs will need to be addressed but what I want to understand is *their* experience. The important thing is how they are trying to learn and gain knowledge that will expose what is and what isn't working for them. The knowledge that such "learning disabled" people have given me has been priceless, and is set out in this book by integrating narrative, processes and personal stories.

A Different Perspective

When you take a different perspective – such as is offered in this book – change can be rapid, although not necessarily the quick fix that many expect from medication. Seeing change in young people and adults is a hugely rewarding experience and one that opens new possibilities, both for our exceptional young people and potentially for improving family life. It is about a journey of discovery and your personal development. As you become more curious further insights will present themselves. You will learn about yourself and how to develop alternative strategies for learning, ones that will prove beneficial to yourself and others. Many of my clients are gifted with a genius level ability to see different perspectives simultaneously; physically, mentally or emotionally. It is my hope that by the end of this book you will be able to see yourself and/or those you care about from a new perspective, one that takes into account their extraordinary skills in a way that can serve them even better.

Through a series of simple skills, this book provides a step by step learning process towards change. The book is designed for those who have lived with SpLDs and are prepared to try something different. Some people have commented that the work I do is so simple, it can't possibly work. Who said change has to be hard? Some of the best discoveries started off as just a hunch. "The world is full of obvious things which nobody by any chance ever observes" according to Sherlock Holmes[3]. In our science-based world, every

issue often seems to have an ever more complex solution. Perhaps this has led us to overlook the obvious!

Working as a family is key to success with SpLDs. When a young person learns a new strategy, they have to practise to become expert. In many instances, however, young people may choose not to do this for a variety of different reasons. In particular, we know how young people may be influenced by friends or other family members who share the same challenge. Perhaps they don't want to let them down or show them up. Therefore, I prefer to work with families. This encourages the development of a healthy, mutual learning environment where children feel empowered to change. Moreover, this allows whole families to learn and grow together. When working with individuals or young people in schools, I ask them to identify who else they can now teach, to reinforce the learning and encourage people to help each other.

You may be tempted to read through the entire book in one sitting. When it comes to learning new skills, however, faster isn't necessarily better. Carry the book with you and repeat the exercises as many times as you need. This will help you experience the full effect, and encourage you to then continue regular maintenance. As time progresses, you will continue to learn from your own experience.

Moving Forward in New Ways

To summarise, this book will help to make you an expert in:

- Helping our talented young people excel.
- Understanding SpLDs from the perspective of the learning differences of the person involved.
- Engaging people with their own experiences and seeing how simple tools can often create rapid change.
- Engaging families; the experts who know their children are bright and who want to be able to help them to learn more easily.
- Assisting families to reduce their stress in the most challenging of circumstances.
- Changing a "common injustice" which results in those exceptional human beings, who simply learn differently, so often struggling with many challenges.
- Seeing how many of the symptoms of SpLDs can be prevented.
- Creating change, success and improved results through integration with existing educational practices.

The audience for this book includes:

- Parents who, with little time or resources, want to really assist their young people to achieve their potential.
- Teachers who want to find new skills to integrate into their classrooms, to help all their pupils achieve, and to make the biggest impact in the time available.

- Medical practitioners who have limited options available to help families.

This work was initially for those with SpLDs; those bright young people who have specific challenges. However the skills covered here are just as appropriate to anyone with any form of learning difficulty, whether they have a diagnosis or not. The content can also contribute to the whole field of Special Educational Needs (SEN) that covers behavioural, learning, physical and hearing challenges. You can just take the structure and information here and develop your own recipes for specific challenges. This book has connected best practice education with the ancient traditions of understanding how the mind, body and spirit work together in a way that anyone can understand. *You* will be able to take this approach further, for those *you* work with.

Although I have used the terminology "young people" and "children" often within this book, everything here is equally applicable and relevant to adults.

"This book introduces concepts that did not ask me to completely re-write the model of my medical world. Instead I could stretch and advance it further". Dr Arti Maini, General Medical Practitioner and Medical Educationalist.

What Could We Achieve Together?

To consider some stark facts:

- 100% of people I have met who are poor at literacy or numeracy have a good to exceptional ability to recall pictures in their mind's eye, and yet have never learnt the skill to visualise words and numbers.

- Letters and words move on the page because of habitual stress. Stop the stress and words will stay still. The same is true for your mind's eye – stop the stress and letters stop moving.
- All good spellers will tell you they can see words in their mind's eye. Why don't we tell every parent and teach it as a simple "how to" skill that everyone can use? It can't do any harm.
- Those with SpLD often have above or well above average IQ. But they are seen - and see themselves - as deficient in some way that they are unable to change.
- Multi-sensory teaching and learning is specified in the National Curriculum in the UK. However, teachers are instructed to teach phonic spellings, and nothing else. They aren't trained in how children learn visually and the mistakes they make, so this really limits their understanding. Visual skills are not even mentioned in the Early Years Foundation Stage[4].
- Young people frequently report letters and words moving or changing places on the page. Just imagine what that would be like all day, every day. Yet it is a simple skill to teach people how to hold the letters still, for themselves, without any external assistance. The first skill you will learn in this book stops this, immediately. Like any new skill you just need to practice.
- When we are very busy, there are numerous thoughts running around in our head. This is confusing for most of us, and as adults we learn to take a break. For young people with SpLDs, such as ADHD, this constant inundation would be their experience all day long.

There are in this book, **how to** skills to change all of the above and more, quickly and at little cost. When these skills are learned and applied they can overcome the symptoms of SpLD permanently. You can be symptom free and retain your exceptional talents.

When this happens, I have already heard people claiming that the diagnosis must have been wrong, rather than accepting that the symptoms can be overcome! There are, however, case studies of people growing out of the negative symptoms of Dyslexia[5], ADHD and Autism[6]. Many young people flounder around with reading to start with and then their teacher says they suddenly "get it." So if some people can grow out of it, we must be able to teach others to do the same.

Imagine for a moment that we could integrate these simple skills into the educational curriculum for our children in their first years at school. Imagine what it would be like for all children to have the skills to learn easily and avoid their deepening confusion. Imagine happier more confident children, less financial cost and emotional stress to parents and schools, improved results, less frustration and conflict, fewer offenders, the list goes on... Imagine how much that would change our classrooms, homes and communities. Isn't this a challenge worth taking, a prize worth fighting for?

Imagine this producing a scenario, where 50% of those with a variety of learning difficulties could find life 10% easier. A further 25% could find learning 50% easier and 90% of four year olds now entering the education system might never reverse their letters, words and numbers, or develop SpLD.

What would this do for our societies worldwide?...

You won't know what you can do until you try and in Paul McKenna's words "You don't have to believe it, just do it."

The processes described in this book are all natural processes with no side effects; I recommend you try them out on yourself first to increase your understanding of them and then help your young people. The only word of caution is not to use them when driving or operating machinery; sometimes they may lead to a relaxed trance-like state which would be unsafe.

PART 1: BACKGROUND

Chapter 1: Rethinking "Learning Difficulties"

Here is the mystery; SpLD can be seen as exceptional talents co-existing with often debilitating symptoms in our intelligent young people. How can we learn to help them reach or exceed their potential?

What are Learning Difficulties?

The umbrella term Specific Learning Difficulty (SpLD)[7] is used to cover a wide variety of difficulties, for example:

- Dyslexia: spelling and reading difficulties.
- Dysgraphia: writing difficulty.
- Dyspraxia: motor difficulties.
- Dyscalculia: a difficulty performing mathematical calculations.
- Attention Deficit Disorder or Attention Deficit Hyperactive Disorder (ADD or ADHD): concentration difficulties with heightened activity levels and impulsiveness.
- Asperger's Syndrome and Autism Spectrum: emotional behaviour or even social communication difficulties.

In addition, Sensory Processing Disorder, Auditory Processing Disorder, Irlen Syndrome[8], Tourette's syndrome and subsets of the above (for example Verbal Dyspraxia) are just some of the ever-increasing list of learning difficulties young people and adults are being diagnosed with. Those diagnosed with SpLD will generally have a severe discrepancy between achievement and intellectual ability.

SpLDs all have their own list of possible symptoms, some of which are quite debilitating. Many of these symptoms overlap with one another, leading to the diagnosis of multiple conditions.[9] In addition, few people have exactly the same combination of SpLDs and some symptoms simply don't easily fit into any one of the many diagnoses.

For simplicity's sake, however, I have summarised the wide variety of SpLD symptoms here as:

- Poor literacy, numeracy and handwriting.
- Visual stress with letters moving on the page.
- Low self-esteem and feelings of withdrawal.
- Daydreaming, involuntary movements.
- Stressed, overload.
- Extreme emotional states even complete "meltdowns."
- Sensitive young people, often having allergies.
- Wobbliness, not knowing where your body is.
- An overactive body that is often, unable to stay still.
- Distracted, lack of concentration.
- Poor motor skills and co-ordination.
- Unbalanced sensory system, affecting visual, auditory, emotional, internal dialogue.
- Challenges with sleep, toilet training etc.
- Poor memory and information processing.
- Poor communication and isolation.

The Problem of Labelling

When you look at the vast range of symptoms that accompany SpLD, it becomes easy to understand how there can be so much overlap between the various diagnoses and why people are diagnosed with a "bit of this" and a "bit of that." The diagnoses just describe a group of symptoms.

In addition, some SpLDs seem to be more about 'being' than 'learning', e.g. ADHD, Autism and Dyspraxia. Learning is more of a secondary problem.

Many talented, creative, capable and successful people are diagnosed with SpLD, however. Where then is the dividing line between the gifted people and those with SpLD? This phenomenon has heightened my concern about the practice of labelling. In A *Boy Beyond Reach*, Dr. Cheri Florance describes her horror at the labelling of her learning challenged son. "I was afraid that if anyone started referring to him as ... handicapped, learning disabled ... or anything, he'd be stuck with that definition ... I wouldn't label him, I would talk about what wasn't working."[10]

Young people I work with who have been "diagnosed" may use it as a defence mechanism, blaming everything on, for example, Asperger's Syndrome and as a result get very stuck. Some of their 'symptoms' may be just normal for a young person

The Limitations of Assessments

In order to go about approaching many very tricky cases of SpLD, it is crucial that we – as both family members and educators – are focused on creating the best possible conditions for effecting change.

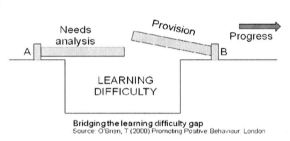

Bridging the learning difficulty gap
Source: O'Brien, T (2000) Promoting Positive Behaviour. London

But as Tim O'Brien's model has pointed out, there currently exists a major disconnection in educational practice between what one could call "needs analysis" and the actual provision of assistance to people with SpLD. Crucially, this disconnection between needs and provision is most glaringly manifest in the assessment process for children suffering with SpLD. Such extensive assessments, available both through the education service or privately, test a young person's performance against norms for the population and identify what they find difficult or easy. Identified deficits are focused on, with the assessor offering a list of recommendations to the school.

Things quickly become more complicated, however. In particular, schools may be unaware of how to deliver on these recommendations, or simply don't have resources to do it. Moreover, some assessments make no attempt to recommend any new skills that the young person can develop. In most instances, the educational system just relies on technology and additional time in exams to support children with SpLD. The assessments I see for clients, however, normally identify the young person as having a high level of visual skills. That said, the assessors rarely ask the young person what their experience of these visual skills is like in different situations.

This book, however, sets out to bridge this disconnection between current modes of learning disability assessment and a child-centred approach to helping the young people develop *new* and effective skills.

Chapter 2: Creativity and SpLD

The Two Contrary Aspects of SpLDs

The expression "yin yang" is used to describe how polar or seemingly contrary forces are interconnected and interdependent in the natural world, and how they give rise to each other in turn.

Likewise, I see the two fundamental aspects of SpLD to be operating simultaneously, much like the yin and the yang. Though SpLD come with a series of obvious downsides – particularly the debilitating symptoms – they are often accompanied by another, quite different set of features, including a range of exceptional skills that such individuals possess.

This reality is easiest to explain through examples. For instance, if you have an exceptional visual skill, such as the ability to visualise fast moving video pictures, then, for instance, this may be great for making up stories. Many dyslexics have these extraordinary skills to move objects about on the page and in their imagination, seeing different perspectives. This skill even spreads into being able to see different sides of an argument very easily. However, doing the same thing with words on a page of course doesn't work, as all the letters fly around and cause confusion. Paradoxically, the more exceptional your super-visual skills, the more confusion they can cause, while those without such exceptional visual skills never move letters around on the page and therefore don't get confused. In addition, fast moving pictures may be excellent for coming up with new ideas, but distracting when you need to focus on a single answer in exams.

This approach to teaching simple skills can be summed up in Bernadette McLean's review of my previous book, *Seeing Spells Achieving*. As McLean writes, "This book teaches visualisation which is a skill that is useful for spelling, reading and also for comprehension. The book does more than work on visualisation techniques, it helps learners replace self limiting beliefs and become 'unstuck' from feelings of failure."[11] Since the publication of that book, I have found additional simple skills that anyone can learn to transform many other symptoms of SpLD.

Exceptional People

There are many well know people in history who had extraordinary talents, and yet judged by today's standards such men and women would have been considered to have SpLDs. For example, Albert Einstein, Winston Churchill and Leonardo da Vinci would all have been subject to such labelling. Things are changing, however. Today it is so supportive to have celebrities such as Richard Branson, Jamie Oliver, Susan Hampshire, Tom Cruise, Whoopi Goldberg, Michael Heseltine, Jeremy Irons, Steve Redgrave, Jackie Stewart and Andreas Panayiotou openly admit to having one or more SpLDs. Unsurprisingly, however, such people are viewed by the public in the light of their *exceptional* skills rather than for their SpLDs. Such men and women were resilient enough to succeed, despite their challenges.

Could young people with SpLDs simply be gifted children who haven't yet discovered their gifts or how to use their gifts? As such, how can we as educators, families and friends help them develop this resilience? Could we in fact help SpLD children to develop more effectively by acknowledging and nurturing their gifts at an early age? In my experience, those with unacknowledged gifts assume everyone else has the same skills, and they rarely believe they themselves are special. Damagingly, the focus is on their deficits rather than on their skills.

Many of the gifts such people have are visual and creative, often revolving around the ability to see things differently. Perhaps unsurprisingly, they possess a range of abilities which are not generally acknowledged in the same way as traditional academic standards. For example, look at the experience of two dyslexics, both of whom possessed exceptional visual skills, but who were incorrectly using the same techniques for words:

David was severely dyslexic in school and is now training to be a mountain guide. When asked why he was doing this he just shrugged his shoulders. His girlfriend said "He's amazing; he never gets lost on mountains." I asked David how he did that and he, in usual nineteen year old parlance, said "Dunno". His girlfriend said, "Ask him about maps." He replied, "Well", taking a deep breath and looking at me as if to say doesn't everyone know this and then said very politely "You know those lines on an Ordnance Survey map which show how steep the mountains are, the contour lines. Well, when I look at a map, the mountains jump up into a 3D picture and I look at the real mountains and it is obvious which way to go." I don't know who was more surprised; David for realising he had a skill others didn't have or me at realising anyone could do that with a map! Now this is exactly what he was doing with letters and letters aren't 3D. Can you imagine what it is like to read words when they are in 3D and moving? An awareness of this and learning the skill of holding the letters still dramatically improved his reading abilities.

Richard, a very good double glazing installer, is now a manager and teaching others his skills. When he looks at a window, his visual memory calculates all the rebates, angles etc. to get a perfect fit. He can literally look at a pile of bits on the floor, cast his eyes over to the window and a bit like Superman looking over his glasses see an instant image of the finished product. He grew up helping his granddad who was a carpenter, so you can guess where he got those skills. He now asks his students whether they can picture the job they are doing in their imagination, and if not teaches the skill.

He learnt how to visualise words using his great visual skills and started practising enthusiastically. It was three months before I met him again as it had been very busy, at the end of the financial year. He was really apologetic and said he just hadn't had time to practice after the first two weeks. Asking him how his spelling was now he said "Well, it's really odd. The spell check on my computer keeps not working, I have had the IT department along twice and they say its fine". In reply I asked him if it was possible he could now spell. He looked astonished and burst out laughing, saying "Do you really think so?" Having realised how to visualise words and keep the letters still, his brain had just made the adjustments and writing customer letters became easy and his career progressed further.

The next is a great example of how an individual's exceptional skills can in fact confuse others. Once understood, the individual became an even better resource for the whole team:

Glen, a very senior Director in an electronics company, could look at a printed circuit board and point out any mistakes in seconds. Again, it was like watching Superman peer over the top of his glasses and run a laser across all the circuits. The only problem was it all happened so fast he had no idea how he came to the decision. His staff wanted more information, but it was gone and he seemed unable to slow down the processing to offer any useful advice. He also realised that all his working instructions were destroyed instantly, he simply said, "Well, it would be too much information to hold in my head, so I just get rid of them." Once he explained this to his team, they could call on his skills and accept his comments.

The final two are about people being able to see different perspectives of the same thing, as if viewing it from a multiple of different directions:

Andy, a manager working in a double-glazing company, found his mind drifted during board meetings. He was always coming up with new ways of doing things and found he struggled to keep focused and explain them. He gave me a fabulous example: as he looked out the window he saw a van parked outside. His brain would go into overdrive, looking at the company logo, turning the letters into 3D objects, moving them around, thinking about the strap line and making up new ones, then considering what van and what colour would be better, etc., etc. All this in just a couple of seconds! Andy wasn't very tall and I had noticed his feet swinging off the floor throughout this conversation. I asked him to relax and get his feet on the floor. "How does the van look now?" "It's just a van, the chaos has stopped and I can concentrate," he replied. Today he would have probably been labelled ADHD, but what a great skill.

Samuel's mum reported that he would hit someone and show no remorse and at the same time he had a deep understanding of people. I asked her to ask him what he visualised. She went home and asked him what image came to him when he was at school and thought of her. He took a deep breath and said "Well... (this was clearly his specialist subject) I see seven mummies, they are all wearing different clothes, they all have different expressions and they are all you." Nobody could have guessed that answer and what an extraordinary skill. Now put yourself in his position; when he hits someone and he can see seven or eight images of them which one is he to take any notice of? Samuel was diagnosed Autistic, but the diagnosis made no mention of this exceptional skill.

There are many other abilities that are often under-appreciated by their owners:

- Proof readers spot typographical errors so easily because they can literally scan a page and any mistakes just "jump out" at them.
- Michael Faraday, the 19th Century physicist, was able to visualise non-visible electromagnetic "lines of force" as clear to him as rubber bands.[12] It was years later that others finally discovered the mathematical formulae to support this. Today you can see this with a magnet and iron filings.

- On You Tube there is a remarkable video of Stephen Wiltshire, the "Human Camera",[13] reproducing all of Rome in great detail after just one trip over it in a plane.

- Fashion designers will often tell you how they can easily imagine a dress that doesn't exist, going on to design it, work out how to construct it, and finish the job. Architects possess similar skills for imagining and constructing buildings.

- Some people in the film industry can play scenes forwards and even backwards in their imagination. They can also edit and re-run it before having to commit to the cutting room floor.

The Creative Skills of Children with SpLD

Creativity in all aspects of life is so important and something that is, in my opinion, grossly under-acknowledged. The child who grows up with creative ideas about how to resolve problems, how to imagine solutions that no-one else thinks of and how to have the resilience to follow through with these ideas, has some of the most important skills for life.

Crucial to creating change, I have found, is harnessing the creativity of children. Those with SpLD seem to have unbounded creativity and divergent thinking, possibly fuelled by their ability to learn differently.

As Sir Ken Robinson[14] has argued, creativity is defined by an ability to think of a lot of ways to interpret a question and to come up with several possible answers, not just one. Crucially, creative people think laterally. From his research, Robinson found that most four year olds measure 98% on levels of creative divergent thinking. As these children grew older, however, their scores dropped – a scientific confirmation that creativity is, in fact, suppressed as children age.

The creative skills mentioned earlier all have some common themes, for example the ability to create good or exceptional pictures in your mind's eye. Your mind's eye is the expression used as a shorthand description for the process by which your brain creates a mental picture of an object or word that you can see by recalling that image from your memory.

Parents and teachers of young children know that they learn through a mixture of their senses. This book mainly focuses on our visual skills. There is, however, a great deal of difference between visual *teaching* and visual *learning*. Showing someone a picture is visual *teaching*. If you tell a story about an imaginary dragon, for example, the whole class may quite rightly make up different pictures of dragons – this is called visual *learning*. When you are teaching a fact like the shape of Africa, they need to see this exactly; but if you tell them precisely what their dragon should look like you are stamping out creativity. I shall always remember the story about a little boy who was continually told to draw in class. Instead of using his imagination, he had to wait for the teacher to draw first and copy it down. He just stopped being creative and no-one noticed until he moved to his next school. All was not lost, though, for his new teacher handed him back permission to use his fabulous imagination. (The Little Boy, Helen E. Buckley)[15]

Visual *learning* is a fabulous skill essential for so many things in life. That said, one of the challenges the class teacher has is that he or she has no idea what pictures have been created in a pupil's mind. The young person will most likely look as if they are in a bit of a trance, focused on this imaginary dragon and seemingly not paying attention to the teacher. How many children do you know who are reprimanded for daydreaming in class? Ask them what they are doing, or what they are seeing and you may in fact find a very creative mind at work. You may have heard a teacher rebuke a child and say "the answer's not on the ceiling." But, for the visual child, that is exactly where they will find the answer.

People with exceptional visual skills in fact have a lot to teach us about the extraordinary way they learn and the skills that gives them. Instead of viewing them as learning deficient, we should recognise their skills and learn from such children. It is my contention that they can potentially provide important messages for parents, teachers and even the whole educational system.

Dr. Kate Saunders, CEO of the British Dyslexia Association, provided this quote for me to publish:

"I was fortunate to have a wonderful mentor and tutor, Dr. Margaret Newton, at the University of Aston, an early pioneer in the Dyslexia field. She diagnosed my own dyslexia in my first year at university and said to me, "We need you in this field, because you will be able to see things that we can't". She empowered me with a sense of responsibility to use my Dyslexic brain to help others within the field, because it works in a different way. Her feeling was that dyslexics can sometimes come at problems from a different direction, think along different routes and that this could lead to solutions that might be of tremendous potential value to the world. I will always be deeply grateful to her for this perspective. In working with dyslexic children for many years now as a teacher and assessor, one of the greatest joys has often been the feeling of standing in awe at the tremendous potential within them. What is often curious to me is that not everyone around the child has noticed this potential."

In my experience, Dyslexics and those with many other SpLDs learn *differently* and do come at things from many different perspectives. Rather than obsess over these children's "deficiencies," it is far more profitable to think about how best to teach those who learn differently and how they are going to make tremendous contributions to the world in the years to come.

Chapter 3: How Do We Learn New Skills?

When we learn a new skill people usually go through the same steps, progressing from novice to proficient. For some, however, the process is not so simple, linear or complete. Understanding the success or failure of this process can tell us much about SpLD, and how best to respond to the particular issues and challenges they present.

The Deficit Paradigm

Current approaches to SpLDs largely operate from a "deficit" paradigm that fails to fully consider all parts of the learning process, including when (and why) it is successful and where it goes wrong. One might wonder, for example, why a young person can't concentrate in school and yet manages to concentrate on their computer game for several hours at a time. The young person has clearly learnt to effectively concentrate in one environment and not another. What exactly is the difference between the two? Another topic of interest might be how some young people can read much better than they can spell.

It is my contention, outlined in this book, that understanding how individuals learn gives you a better appreciation of which aspects of the learning process are contributing to a young person's learning difficulty. Adding to this a best practice approach to finding out how young people who are successful achieve this success gives you all the keys you need. Put together, this knowledge can effectively reveal the source of the problem and go a long way towards helping parents and educators address the issue.

The "deficit" paradigm currently in ascendance within SpLD circles rests on the assumption that something is wrong with the individual and that they are unable do something that most other children can achieve with ease. When you come from this point of view, it is perhaps natural to focus on research into why these young people can't do something. Most current studies are focusing on issues such as brain deficits and genetics, while assessing the children against norms in the population. Researchers' findings have led to an educational philosophy that tends to over-teach the very thing that isn't working. Repetitive practice of the same things may work for some, but will not for many others.

My approach comes from a different perspective, taking a holistic approach to the learning process to access the root causes of the SpLD. I employ knowledge of the exceptional skills young people possess for learning other things and the ways in which they learn in different circumstances. I also collect knowledge about how others have made substantive changes in order to accelerate the process for the next young person with a similar challenge.

How People Learn

To understand the mechanics of the learning process, you must first understand the basics of the conscious and unconscious mind. To keep things simple, you can think of your conscious mind containing all the thoughts you are aware of. In addition to this, there is much more going on in your unconscious mind, which is running the show. Your conscious mind is just aware of the tip of the iceberg – perhaps only 5%; there is much more under the water in your unconscious mind (95%) that is much less obvious.

As we learn a new skill or ability, it starts as a very conscious activity. Only over time does it transfer to an unconscious habit. As human beings learning new skills, we pass through the four learning stages outlined below[16].

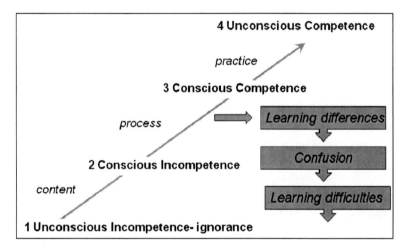

Stage 1: Unconscious Incompetence: A state of ignorance. Not only do you not know how to do something; you also don't know what you don't know.

Stage 2: Conscious Incompetence: You know that you don't know how to do something. You need to learn the all important **how to** skill; the capability.

Stage 3: Conscious Competence: You know how to do something and you need practice to become proficient.

Stage 4: Unconscious Competence: You are able to do something skilfully, without needing to consciously pay attention. It has become a habit.

To illustrate this process, consider the example of learning to drive. When we are born, we are in **Stage 1**, with no idea there is such a skill to learn. At the time of our first driving lesson we have arrived at **Stage 2**, wherein everything seems very complicated and confusing. At this stage, there are several skills to learn and much co-ordination is needed between looking at the road, starting the engine and breaking. When we take a driving test we are (hopefully!) at **Stage 3** and we know exactly what to do in any given situation. After a few years of driving the whole thing becomes much more automatic, and we no longer concentrate on the details anymore. At this point, our driving abilities have reached **Stage 4**.

The process works in exactly the same manner for children's education in school. In its most successful form, some young people may learn things in the classroom so quickly that you may even see young children jumping from Stage 1 to Stage 4, without apparently passing through any of the intervening stages.

Think for a moment about how you have learnt and become competent in some of your habits.

Things We Learn Without Being Taught

Some skills, however, do not need to be explicitly taught for us to pick them up effectively. We go through exactly the same steps as above, but without any formal training. I call these "natural skills."

Learning to walk, for example, is achieved both though the

inspiration and encouragement of others and also through a trial and error strategy that continues until the child becomes competent. There is no formal training manual about how limbs move, or which muscles you have to use. Children see other people walking and eventually try it out for themselves. The first time a child falls over, he or she will just try again. Rarely does the child give up for any extended period of time. Although learning to walk is a very visible skill, and one that parents helps their child with, in large part the child has to actually work it out for themselves: a "natural skill."

Learning to talk is another "natural skill". We have found instances when too much correction, offered by the kindest of parents, can offend a child and they give up for a period of time. It is best to just ignore any mistakes in the early days, and they will pick up the basics naturally, correcting themselves over time.

Most of the skills that this book explains are in fact such "natural skills". That said, the reality is that although some children learned these naturally and easily, many others did not. For many children, their inability to pick up such "natural skills" has affected the trajectory of their whole educational experience; this is too important to leave to chance.

For those who struggle with SpLD, one of the most important "natural skills" to learn is the ability to be able to visualise and have control over your visual memory. Two young people in the same family can both have great visual memories for pictures. Whereas one uses it effectively to visualise words, learning to read and spell, the other will often have no idea what you are talking about. One will excel in the classroom, whereas the other will often be struggling mightily at school. Visualising words is just one of the "natural skills" that very few people are taught. This book teaches you many of the "natural skills" that are so critical to avoiding confusion and learning effectively.

All of these skills can be taught in school to very young children. Indeed, the younger the better! If you teach them these "natural skills", you aren't leaving it to chance that the child will naturally pick them up. In many respects, the teaching of such "natural skills" is a fantastic preventative measure that can save much time, energy and money in the long run. They only take minutes, for example:

- Creating focus, a calm environment and releasing stress.
- Visualising words and numbers and keeping them still (needed for literacy and mental maths).
- Adjusting the position of work to minimise any feelings of failure
- Sequencing visually.
- Reducing the feeling of being overwhelmed.
- Copying down from the board and improving handwriting.
- Copying down from their visual memory to paper.
- Converting stories into picture memories (essential for comprehension).
- Converting lists and instructions into picture memories (short term memory).
- Converting pictures and thoughts into the written word (story writing).
- Creating imaginary pictures.
- Improving concentration, attention, listening skills and controlling a movie memory to create still pictures.
- Learning how to "let go" of negative emotions.

Once you identify skills people need you can see clearly how they can be taught, when younger, in a way that avoids confusion developing.

Parents can really assist with all of these skills in simple ways, and getting other family members involved can be very beneficial.

Chapter 4: The Child-Centred Approach to Learning

Child-centred learning is an approach to education focusing on the needs, abilities, interests and learning styles of the child, rather than those involved in the educational process, such as teachers and administrators.

Who Is the Expert?

Child-centred learning means putting the students at the centre of the learning process. It will, for example, strengthen motivation, reduce disruptive behaviour, build child-teacher relationships and promote active learning – in short, you will be talking their language. For SpLD the child-centred approach is critical for any teacher to understand why a child is having difficulties and where their strengths lie.

Symptom based diagnosis cannot fully address the particular problems that emerge from a child's difficulties with the learning process. Rather, the only way we can really find out about SpLD is to ask the child themselves. The child is the expert on their own experience and the only person who knows exactly what happens. This is their normal state of being and one that they live with constantly. All too often, they may not realise there is another way to be. Even if they do, they may not possess the communication skills necessary to explain why and how they do what they do.

Thus, what I and others call "child-centred development and learning" is at the heart of my approach to those struggling with

SpLD. Indeed, child-centred development is key to many initiatives, including those of The United Nations Children's Fund (UNICEF).

An individual may not currently be in possession of all the skills needed and as long as a certain amount of progress can be made, that individual can use their own intelligence and talents to develop further.

Learning from Others

Neuro-linguistic Programming (NLP) is the study of experience and excellence; how and why do people do the things they do? NLP has done much work on modelling behaviour. When you discover how one person does something well, you can model that and teach others to do the same. Once we have an understanding of how 'unchallenged' learners learn, we can pass on that knowledge and teach it to the 'challenged'.

We have gained brilliant insights that we can teach to others, from:

- Adults explaining what happened in childhood; things they could never have explained at the time.
- Engaging the child and the child's closest relatives about their experience.
- Adults who exhibit some of these symptoms from time to time have explained how they change states so easily, whereas those with SpLD spend most of their time in these unhelpful states.
- Knowledge of the brain.

They have provided me with valuable insights that have added to my understanding of the experiences that young people have. We can't have a child-centred approach without asking the young person what is going on.

When we know something that can help, it is our responsibility as adults to offer it to others – to individuals, families and teachers. We all want to do the best we can for our young people.

> I remember the delightful nine year old I met in Holland who after learning to spell visually in less than an hour turned around and said "This is all too easy – isn't it cheating?".

Bringing Together Patterns

Once you start using the child-centred approach you start to see patterns for the challenges. These patterns indicate shortcuts to use what works for individuals and teach it to others or groups – a "recipe" that can be used by the whole family. As you progress in this book, you will find and begin to develop unique recipes for your specific requirements. You will be able to adjust them as you wish, however, as they represent just the starting point for learning and discovery.

This book will give you a core set of tools. As you become proficient with these tools you will start making your own recipes. The best 'master chef,' however, is you. In almost all cases, it is the parent who is best positioned to take the tools and use them with their young person's specific needs in mind.

A Little Detective Work

It is invaluable to understand what is happening from the individual's perspective without judgement. Indeed, if parents or educators go jumping into an individual's predicament, everyone may get stuck! I don't need to know what happens in terms of a child's behaviour, whether it is at home or in school. Rather, I am primarily interested in what is *causing* the behaviour.

As such, being curious with clients and their problems has become a particular focus of mine and taught me much of what I know today. Children suffering with SpLD will, at some level, know exactly what is happening to them. Many, however, will have no idea how to explain their difficulties or how to change them. To fully help young people, therefore, it is essential that they are able to tell you about their own confusion and whenever possible talk with people without SpLD about their experience too, to give you a contrast.

When observing a young person and their difficulties, you may find the following questions helpful:

- What are they really good at? Get them on their specialist subject.
- What can you notice about an individual's experience? What are they telling you about their experience?
- What is your intuition telling you? What are you observing?
- From the child's perspective, what is this behaviour like? What are they getting from this behaviour?

- What are they telling you in casual conversation about their map of the world, the paradigm in which they live? Be observant, it is unlikely to be the same as yours.
- What is causing them to be most and least productive?
- Be curious, asking questions like "how do you do that", "how does that work", or "is that a good strategy"?

You may find it useful to start by attempting to understand your own experience, in particular how and why you exhibit the behaviours that you do. We may see in others the challenges we also have. The key is to be curious and attempt to learn together. I mentioned earlier that we can all exhibit some of the symptoms of SpLD from time to time. Being curious about how adults change between these two states offers us techniques to teach others.

What Does the Client Want?

The next thing to understand is "what does the client want?" Are they motivated to do what their parents want? The common requirement from parents is for children to be able to reverse some of the symptoms outlined earlier and do better in school. For young children the themes are similar, but by the time they get a little older they will have their own views. For example, if they don't want to learn to read there is nothing you can do to insist they do. You have to find some way to motivate them. See Chapter 9: *What holds you back?*

Chapter 5: When Things Go Wrong

Once you have understood your child's particular experiences and reality you can begin to understand how and why the learning process goes wrong. The learning process may get stuck in confusion; children (and adults) may learn limiting beliefs or some may get very attached to not being able to do something. This chapter will give you insights into what is really happening.

Stuck in Confusion

A little confusion is a natural thing when you are learning a new skill, triggering an opportunity to adapt and grow. It is not somewhere you want to be stuck for too long, however.

I see many young people become consciously incompetent and get stuck there. This is almost always because their learning style is fundamentally *different* to the way they are being taught. Stuck in the middle of stages 2 and 3, such children become surrounded by confusion. Here are a few examples that illustrate the point:

- In the process of learning to drive, some people become frightened, embarrassed, uncoordinated or find it difficult to follow instructions as the instructor doesn't explain in a way that makes any sense.

- Young people will often be excited about learning to read for a period of time, but succumbing to confusion for any extended time de-motivates them and they may then seem lazy or disruptive.
- Having learnt to walk, you may go to a swimming pool. You could just walk, treading water and become very confused about why you can't go very fast. You are just using the wrong strategy, it would be better to learn to swim.
- Without the skill to visualise still words, literacy will be restricted.

This confusion and stress will, over a period of time, result in identified SpLD. The key to solving these problems, then, is to determine what is causing the confusion. As this book will show, in order to help children who learn differently, we need to help teach some important, practical **"how to"** skills.

Confusion only amplifies over time. For example, not knowing which way round a letter goes at the age of four to six may develop into rotating whole words such as **was** and **saw** within a couple of years. If such problems persist, this can lead to words moving all over the page by the age of eleven and the beginnings of clear, identifiable Dyslexia. As these confusion-related issues deepen, you will also see a widening gap between the young person and their peers and the possibility of deteriorating behaviour. This confusion alongside increasing frustration can lead to disaffected young people becoming young offenders. Moreover, I have seen adult dyslexics, so exhausted by trying to make sense of letters and words moving before their eyes, develop Chronic Fatigue, or even mental health issues, later in life.

Limiting Beliefs are Very Powerful

Limiting beliefs can also have a big impact on the development and deepening of SpLD. Put simply, limiting beliefs are any belief you develop that limits your abilities. Beliefs develop from experiences; they may or may not be true and we can certainly change them if we choose. By contrast, whether you think you can do something or whether you think you can't, either way you are likely to be right – and we do like to be right!

The first is an empowering belief, the second a limiting belief.

Prior to the age of six, it is easy for us to pick up other people's beliefs, especially from figures of authority. In a school setting, authority figures such as teachers can dramatically influence our beliefs about ourselves. If you are told you are stupid, tone deaf or lazy – and take on that belief – you will probably live up to the label. Rather than being taught **how to**, children drop into "I can't". Others may fight to prove the teacher wrong and develop an enormous resilience, refusing to accept what they have been told.

One of the most damaging limiting beliefs is that people are increasingly viewing SpLD as genetic. The popular understanding of this scientific explanation views SpLD as something that can't be changed. As such, this prevents people from looking for other possibilities, and often leads to unhealthy family relations with children blaming their parents for their afflictions. (See chapter 11 for more information on family connections.)

The Identity Jump

We may come into this world believing that anything is possible, but our early experiences tell us that isn't always the case. In many cases, children quickly develop limiting beliefs that become manifest in their self-perception. For example, when a child spills a glass of orange, someone may inform them that they are stupid. Once they've heard this a few times, this can develop into a belief reinforcing this part of a child's self awareness. So the human brain jumps from a *behaviour* to an *identity* very easily. I call this the "Identity Jump". How many times do you hear a parent saying the child is stupid (identity), for just spilling a glass of orange (behaviour). You aren't stupid most of the time. This can often be responsible for the over-reaction we see in children and adults, as it really hurts to have your identity challenged for a relatively minor event.

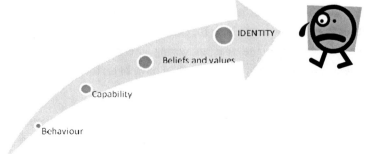

There are some people, however, who grow up with large amounts of psychological resilience and don't let such events bother them. This has much to do with your self esteem, which is also often a crucial aspect of how SpLDs develop.

Self Concept and Self Esteem

Almost everyone with SpLDs has at some time, if not permanently, suffered from poor self esteem. Unhappily, life seems to get increasingly tough at just the time when a child wants everything to be fun. Making things worse, many young people feel they are always wrong. For many children with developing SpLD, praise is often neglected in favour of just making it through the day. These are just some of the earliest challenges to children's self esteem.

It is useful to distinguish between *self concept* and *self esteem*. *Self concept* is how you perceive who you really are. We are unconsciously motivated to manifest our self concept, so it is important to have a positive and solid belief and understanding. *Self esteem*, however, is the evaluation of how well you are doing at manifesting your self concept at any moment[17]. The goal is to have a strong self concept to feel secure, letting your self esteem move up and down, as you evaluate how you are doing in life.

When an individual reports low *self esteem*, they are often overlooking *self concept*. Simply identifying and separating self concept and self esteem can be hugely beneficial. Think of bolstering a young person's self concept in simple everyday life. Who are they? What makes them special? The stronger and better their self concept, the easier they will find it to increase their self esteem. In addition, recognising all those amazing talents that are mentioned in earlier chapters will bolster their self concept, making them more resilient.

Positive By-products

"Human behaviour is purposeful, even though at times what you are doing may seem unwanted, negative or self-destructive. It must have something going for it, some payoff; otherwise you wouldn't be doing it. The secret of changing is to incorporate the positive by-products of your present behaviour into the change you are wishing to make and therefore minimise resistance from within different parts of yourself[18]."

One of the central questions parents and educators should ask about children with SpLD is "what are they getting from their behaviour?" If a parent doesn't like a young person's behaviour, they need first to understand the positive by-products that the young person is getting as a result of their behaviour.

The benefits may include a whole range of things, including more attention, getting their own way, getting time out of class to work with their friends or even feeling affinity with a sibling or parent. By the time they have reached secondary school (11-18 years), poor literacy is very frustrating and at this level you are getting more and more help in school, extra time in exams, or even a free computer – all rather positive by-products. Eventually, this pattern can lead to teenagers sitting back and expecting their Teaching Assistant to do the work for them, even though they are trying – in vain – to keep the young person empowered.

Positive by-products have much to do with conundrums like, "Why do some people practise new skills, whilst others don't?" You won't know the answer to this question until you ask the client. Indeed, there could be several reasons all interacting with one another. For example, children may feel scared at having to do something new, it may remind them of not being able to do something previously, their dad may have the same problem, they may have a limiting belief about what is possible and not want to fail, or they may not have enough time. Many, in fact, just do not want to change.

Considering the reasons behind children's SpLD is crucial because helping a child who is scared of what his friends might say is very different from helping a young person who feels his learning difficulty represents a common bond with his dad.

Given the essentially *individual* nature of a child's SpLD, the prescriptions offered in this book can and should, be tailored to specific cases. As a start, however, this book covers the most common root problems that often eventually manifest themselves as SpLD. That said, I am sure you will find more when you try understanding the world from the young person's point of view and understand their personal positive by-products.

The following questions may be useful to ask your child and consider in your particular learning situation:

- What is this behaviour doing for me/you?
- What are you getting from this behaviour?
- What happens, directly or indirectly when I/you do this?
- What do I /you get from doing this?
- What else do I /you get from doing this?
- What of this is worth keeping?

The repetitive question, "and what is that doing for you?" can often help people to really understand their own behaviour. Once you start really understanding someone else's experience and start thinking differently, insights come tumbling in. Take the following example:

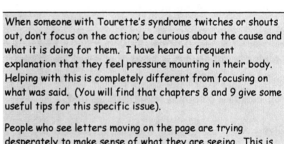

When someone with Tourette's syndrome twitches or shouts out, don't focus on the action; be curious about the cause and what it is doing for them. I have heard a frequent explanation that they feel pressure mounting in their body. Helping with this is completely different from focusing on what was said. (You will find that chapters 8 and 9 give some useful tips for this specific issue).

People who see letters moving on the page are trying desperately to make sense of what they are seeing. This is probably formed from a repetitive thought pattern about "when confused, turn it round", like they did with bricks when they were very young. Turning around 3D objects like bricks is useful; moving 2D letters around is quite useless for words and just causes confusion.

It has been shown that in autistic children their mirror neurons are not working in the same way as in non-autistic people[19]. As autistic people are overwhelmed by too much information, is this nature's way of limiting the amount of information they receive?

Chapter 6: Empowering People to Change

Many parents feel they don't know how to help; they know what they want for their children, but don't know **how to** achieve it. Sometimes individuals are so overwhelmed by all the symptoms that it may be difficult to know where to start; this is where the recipes can really help. Complex problems *can* have very simple solutions.

Now that you understand more about what is happening to young people with SpLDs, the next step towards helping them transform their SpLD is to realise that *you* are the ideal person to help them. As my doctor once said to me, "*You* are the expert on *your* child." The time to start is now; you won't know what they can do until you try! Once you get started, you will be surprised how easily change happens.

Where Do You Start?

As I have learned through my work with clients, people have a lot more choice than they often think. It is very scary with any challenge not to feel in control and able to choose one's actions. Developing the simple skills, outlined in this book, will give them further insights and who knows what they can achieve. Without these tools for change they are likely to be stuck in a rut for a long time with symptoms compounding on top of one another.

Take this example of a family who were trapped in an "impossibility loop." Not knowing which way to turn and resigned to their situation, the family found some simple **how to** skills which changed the lives not just of the children but of the mother as well.

"My sons are both diagnosed Asperger's and ADHD. Since learning the Empowering Learning visualisation techniques the change in the boys has been remarkable. After six years of constant battles and resistance to the concept of having to sit down to learn words, there is now no reluctance to participate in the learning; this in itself is a great and very welcome relief to the whole family. Words are being learnt, remembered and recalled in a relaxed and easy manner; gone are so many of the frustrations. Both boys have progressed from only being willing to learn an agreed six words from the school spellings list to the full list of twenty and, as such, now participate fully with the rest of their class. I am so pleased and amazed by the progress that they have made; these simple but powerful techniques have certainly been the keys to unlock this area of learning for them and help me keep calmer too." Amy

There are many skills you will learn in this book that are simple and easily mastered with just a little practice. Change does not have to be difficult! Some ideas seem to lead to complicated solutions. This book, on the other hand, offers very simplistic ideas. Some you may say are too simplistic, yet they have all worked for others. I'd ask you to suspend judgement, try them for yourself and then decide.

This book proposes that we get young people and families in touch with the skills they already have and help them to make the most effective use of them. The best approach to SpLD empowers individuals, their families and educationalists, who appreciate that no two people are the same. Understanding how a child learns is imperative to help them be successful.

These are simple skills – mainly based on the power of imagination – that can be taught in the classroom. Most young children, in fact, are already expert in using their imagination![20] The Latin word for doctor mean "to teach", highlighting that in this instance the "therapy" of helping a child or adult with SpLDs critically involves *learning* a new approach. This can be taught by parents, teachers, health professionals and anyone wanting to assist. I even encourage small children as young as eight years old to teach each other; they are often great teachers, because they understand the difficulty. For example, holding a book in a different position may help a child to read better and more fluently – this comes from understanding how the brain works, not therapy.

The skills outlined in the rest of the book provide a tool kit for life, one that contains many helpful options and possibilities. You need to find the best tools for you, however. It is how you adapt and use them within your own particular environment that is the real prize. "... apply them to your own expertise to create something new and extraordinary."[21]

These tools will give you a framework, but they are just a starting point. I fully encourage you to add other simple skills applicable to your specific environment and your own particular needs.

To begin with, it is advisable to choose processes that can be used every day. You may find yourself wanting to re-read chapters to give yourself a deeper and clearer understanding of your own experience and those you help. In addition, the best thing to do is to practise on yourself initially, as understanding your own experience will give you the confidence to teach others. However, you may find that those you help have, for example, better visual skills than you do. Don't let this deter you; being visual is our young people' specialist subject. Don't let your own beliefs about your skills limit them.

William, in Chapter 11, learnt a limiting strategy to visualise words all around his head. It worked well for short words, but, as he got older and the words grew longer, it failed so he got confused and dropped into an SpLD. SpLDs are an unconscious competence, you keep doing the same thing and you get the same results, even if that isn't what you really want.

Our job as adults and teachers is to help people find choice when they are stuck, whether it is just a simple suggestion of "how would it be if you could see all of the word" and ask what happens. Only sometimes you may need to ask them something deeper.

Steps for Change

Everyone can do something now! One of the real benefits of this approach is that anyone can pick up valuable skills very rapidly. We can help those we know, without waiting for anything, including new government initiatives. We are in fact only helping people to consciously understand their own experience.

Here are a few practical steps that will help an individual and their family begin to create meaningful change in their lives:

1. **Motivation.** People need to be clear about what would improve if they learned new skills as opposed to remaining as they are. What could your life look, sound, feel like? What would others say/think about you? It is essential to see the benefit to motivate change.

2. **Ask yourself this question: Is there anything stopping you?**
   Sometimes there are things which stop people making changes. In the case of SpLDs, it may be family members, friends at school, teachers or simply the developed belief that they are stupid. Having a family member or friend with a similar challenge can be a real barrier to change, as children may at some level not want to show others up. But when you can engage the family member or friend in the same process of learning, it can prove a powerful team effort.

3. **What do you like doing?** When helping people change, find out what they're good at and what they like doing. This will help them engage in the process. For example, if they are obsessed by dinosaurs, then the first words I teach are dinosaur words. Similarly for football players,

Pokémon characters etc.

4. **Getting into a "learning state" that is grounded:** This is essential for enhancing your focus and concentration. When you are un-grounded you will find it hard to sit still and your sensory, autonomic nervous and immune systems will all be compromised.

5. **Visualising pictures and videos (Appendix A will assist you - and you will probably find that anyone with SpLDs is already expert in this).** The human brain can do both 'stills' and 'moving' visualisations, although, in rare cases, traumas may have shut these pictures away. I teach people to be grounded, feel strongly connected to the planet, release negative emotions and take control over their internal visual pictures – where they are, whether they are moving, what size, colour etc. There are no right answers; they are your pictures and taking control of them aids concentration.

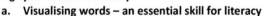

6. **Once you have control over your visual memory, you can experiment with all the things you can learn visually:**
    a. **Visualising words – an essential skill for literacy**
    b. **Visualising numbers – an essential skill for numeracy**
    c. **Improving reading**
    d. **Improving writing and easy ways to copy down from the board**
    e. **Improving short term memory and sequencing**
    f. **Plus ideas you can make up for yourself**

7. **PRACTISE, PRACTISE, PRACTISE, UNTIL YOU FORM NEW HABITS AND PATTERNS.** It may take twenty-eight days to really master a new habit though for some people it may be a lot less. Just 10 minutes daily practice will be effective and try to make practice as much fun as possible. If any negative emotions arise, just send them down into the ground or off to the moon and substitute new confidence.

I have worked in several schools, coaching teachers to learn more about how young people learn visually, and integrating these skills into the classrooms of schools, especially at primary level.

Some people are shocked that change can be so rapid, or as one eight years old in the Netherlands said in a workshop, "This (the simple skills outlined in this book) is too easy – isn't it cheating?" When people find out how to do the many things in history that people thought were miracles, they are no longer miracles.

Teaching these "natural skills" to those under seven and engaging their parents and teachers in understanding the skills their young people need to develop has been found to be the most successful combination. See this reflected in the following Head teacher's words:

"St Alban and Stephen Infant School is a good school but we are always striving to improve. In particular we look for ways to enhance learning, especially for those children who may struggle with literacy and numeracy. We have always used visual, aural and kinaesthetic methods with young children, but we have been shown a number of activities which can really support visual learners and this has been a great step forward. Olive Hickmott has taught our teachers and teaching assistants how children learn visually and how sometimes children confuse themselves. She has shown the staff how to integrate their new skills into the classroom, adding to their Continuous Professional development. Olive has individually taught a few children who have been particularly challenged and coached my staff who have seen for themselves the real benefits of visual learning, being grounded and letting go of stress. We are now developing the ideas into our reception class teaching with the objective that all children build an excellent multi-sensory foundation for literacy and numeracy from the very start". Paula Holden, Head teacher.

PART 2:
SIMPLE SKILLS

Chapter 7: The Essential Energetic Background

Now we are going to move on to the **how to** tools that will begin to help you deal with a range of debilitating symptoms. I have mentioned that I help people understand their own experience. One aspect of this is to understand your energy system and how it has a significant effect on all forms of SpLD.

Principles of Your Body's Energy

As I have discovered in my work with clients, most people with SpLD are very affected by energy. Indeed, parents will often mention that they are "very sensitive young people". When you pick up energy from others, you may act out of that energy as opposed to your own, behaving as the other person would, rather than yourself. People pick up other, external forms of energy in much the same way as people pick up smells when they enter a smoky room; although you eventually leave the smoky surroundings, the smell will go with you and linger on your clothes. It is essential that children and adults learn to clear such foreign energy from their system! Consider this a personal hygiene course for your energy system!

We all know more about energy than we realise. Energy is one of those things we take for granted until we don't have enough of it. For example, we don't notice gravity but without it we would not exist. Indeed, there are many other energy systems at work in the world, including:

- The wind – generally you can't see it (unless it's a tornado and you see collected dust and debris), but you can certainly feel it.
- Electricity – you can't see it and for safety reasons you certainly don't want to feel it.
- Magnetic energy – you will be familiar with lines of magnetic energy going through and around a magnet.
- Mobile phones, which work through transmitting sound in the form of energy.

Likewise, the *human energy* system is present everywhere, both in each cell of our body and around the outside of us. Just considering our own energy system:

- If you have no energy, you simply can't function and your brain is in a fog[22].
- Can you sense the energy of the person sitting next to you? When you travel in a crowded train this can be quite uncomfortable.
- Rub your hands together, feel the energy between them like an imaginary ball; it is no more difficult than feeling the wind on your face, you may just not be used to it.
- If you have someone negative in your life, you may be picking up their energy. You can choose not to keep them in your life or learn how to manage your own energy and not let theirs affect you.
- When you get angry or frustrated, you access energy from previous events which you have been carrying around with you; this can make you feel tired – effectively blowing your fuses.
- You have a body full of energy and like Christmas tree lights[23], when one goes out, others often follow.

- We wash our faces and clean our teeth daily. If you had never washed your hands, they would be very dirty.

To aid your understanding of how energy works and what it does, three basic principles are helpful:

- The first principle is that energy follows thought and your intention. There are a number of books written – such as Lynne McTaggart's "The Field[24]" –scientifically documenting that thoughts have an energetic power and those thoughts can affect people, places and even machines. If you imagine something happening with energy, it will invariably start happening. Simple and true.

- The second principle is that we all have energy centres distributed throughout our body and our energy field. Strong emotions such as anger, frustration, past traumatic experiences and a reaction to our own SpLDs can block our energy channels and in turn affect our health. Energy blocks can be extremely painful. Conscious realisation of these blocks offers a great opportunity for us to clear these energy channels and energetic centres in our entire energy system. You won't know what you can achieve until you try.

- The third principle, which some people find harder, is the usefulness of being playful with energy. Just play with your energy in the way that a child would. Indeed, adopting the persona of a five year old frees your conscious and your unconscious mind, allowing you to really work with your energy.

It is only your conscious mind that has beliefs and programming restrictions.

- The fourth principle is that the more judgmental we are, the more energy we give to the situations we don't like. However bad the situation we find ourselves in, releasing judgment will avoid inflaming the energy we don't like.

Making up images, metaphors or stories is the best way to get access to the subconscious where much of the behaviours known as SpLD reside. Guided imagery is used to create the images, so you can just listen to and join in with a story. It doesn't matter whether you see the images in a story clearly, holographically, in 3D, just sort of vaguely see them or even just pretend, any of these will work.

You will learn how to simply and easily move your energy and maximise your learning skills. Most of the stories are gifts from Art Giser[25], Creator of Energetic NLP. To be most effective, read the story a couple of times and then run through it from memory or order a CD[26]. Some people prefer to listen to a CD so that they can concentrate on their own internal experience. You are welcome to customise the stories with your own metaphors that work better for you or your family. You can choose to use the children's examples or make them up yourself, using the key points. Don't be surprised if you find yourself yawning, sneezing or your eyes watering – this is all part of the energy clearing process. Big yawns – a great indication that you are releasing energy – are a particularly good sign.

Preparing to Affect Your Energy

A few things to help you prepare for the exercises:

- ✓ Sit quietly and comfortably, feet flat on the floor, arms and legs uncrossed and your back fairly straight.
- ✓ Just use your imagination. Don't be concerned about what is real or not. Think about this as being metaphorical. Play with metaphors, to make them work for you.
- ✓ The important thing is to not take them too seriously. When we take them seriously, we try prematurely to decide what is the truth and what is not and that only gets in the way. If you feel the energy flow, that's great and if you don't, that's also great[27].

The Remaining Sections of This Book

The rest of Part 2 gives you a much better understanding of your own experience and some basic skills to try out first and learn more about your own experience and that of your family members. By the end of part 2 you will be well on your way to creating change.

Part 3 has more advanced processes that cover specific challenges, for example Dyslexia, Asperger's, literacy and numeracy skills.

It is important to understand that these chapters are intended to work organically together, one feeding off of another.

Looking at how these chapters interact specifically, people who have a variety of SpLD seem to have just manifested emphasis on different parts of this circle. For example, blocks to success will cause you to be more un-grounded and hence to have more difficulty stabilising your sensory system, which is essential for learning.

- Someone with Dyslexia will not recall words easily (visual sensory system) and will be a little un-grounded.
- Someone with Dyspraxia may have major energy blocks and hence be un-grounded.
- Someone with ADHD will be very un-grounded and may not have energy blocks at all.

This gives us a model to work from about how many of the SpLD seem interlinked.

You will notice that every section in this book has:

- Threads from different clients and stories from specific clients that are a great learning resource.
- Simple instructions for new skills which have worked for others and helped them change.
- A step by step approach. Practise these skills and make the gradient as shallow as you like building on success. You want incremental progress.
- Ideas for helping very young children to grow up with the skills they need to avoid confusion, or at least to have choice.

One role of this book is to point out these connections, giving the reader ideas for changes that can be made to his/her own experience.

Chapter 8: Focus; a Central Component of Learning

As any school teacher would agree, learning is impossible without focus and concentration. What most schoolteachers will not know, however, is that the ability to "ground" oneself is a major contributor to achieving a state of effective learning. Though some people find it easy to be naturally grounded, others need to work at getting into that state.

Different States: "Lose Control and Flap About" or "Keep Calm and Carry On."

A common expression, as you may have heard, is "being in a bit of a state". A state can be thought of as a snapshot of how you are at any particular time. Most people can recall the state of being confused, overwhelmed, unable to focus, having too much stuff going on in or around your head. In simple terms, this is an "un-grounded" state. In fact, many SpLD symptoms are related to being ungrounded, some of which might sound familiar to you:

- Daydreaming, being in a daze or not really here, "spaced out".
- A racing mind – overloaded by thousands of thoughts, with too much going on in or above your head.
- Finding it difficult to articulate thoughts, being unclear.

- Arguing, yet unable to convey your argument clearly.
- Lack of balance – clumsiness, lack of co-ordination, wobbly, losing core stability, walking on toes – like a " Weeble" toy[28].
- Wriggling, being unable to relax, irritable, in perpetual motion, "uncomfortable in your own skin," "ants in your pants." Children's feet might be in the air or up the side of chairs and are often anywhere but on the floor.
- Heart palpitations.
- Static shocks.
- Confusion, forgetful, lack of focus and concentration.
- Regular stressful emotions, feeling nervous, manifesting that familiar "fight, flight or freeze symptom."
- Feeling sick or dizzy.
- Hearing may range from poor to oversensitive.
- Sight may be inconsistent, oversensitive and your mind's eye stuck in uncontrollable fast moving videos, which compete for your attention.

- Speech may falter, stutter, be inconsistent
- Speech may revert to speaking very fast, in a childish manner or even in another voice
- Lacking feelings and disliking being touched.
- There is limited or no access to your internal dialogue (small warning voice in the head), leading to inappropriate behaviour and danger.
- Some bodily systems may not seem to function well; the autonomic nervous system (bodily signals such as needing to

drink water, stop eating or urinating) may be affected, your immune system or circulation.

- Lack of co-ordination and strength, averse to sport
- Children resorting to head banging
- Behaving inappropriately whether physically, verbally and emotionally, possibly because of a lack of a developed internal dialogue.
- Twitching or worse, symptoms that may develop into Tourette's over a period of time
- Flickering eyes, as they recall fast moving videos.
- Flapping about.
- Laughing although things don't seem funny.
- Angry and in some cases completely overreacting to relatively minor things.

In short, being un-grounded is akin to driving a bus whilst sitting on the roof; exciting but not exactly effective!

Grounding is a fundamental "natural skill" that is available to every living creature. It is part of being present on the planet, "your membership card of planet Earth.[29]" When a seed germinates it puts roots down into the earth. Through these pass nutrients and energy for growth while waste products return to the earth for re-cycling. As the seed grows stronger, a shoot grows into the air where it accesses the sun's energy and universal energies. This process continues as it grows perhaps into a plant, perhaps into a tree. Trees are extremely grounded with extensive root systems. Just leaning on a tree can help you ground too. Animals are generally extremely grounded and love a grounded calm environment. There are more details about physical grounding in Appendix B.

What does it feel like when you are grounded? Unsurprisingly, it is almost the opposite of all the above. You will notice:

- Your head is clearer.
- Feeling relaxed and calm.
- Feeling like you.
- Feeling that you can concentrate, take decisions and focus on the task in hand.
- Being strong and centred.

Grounding is even believed to improve blood flow, a central biological function that affects every aspect of your life.

Simple Skill #1: Grounding Yourself

Grounding is all part of a young person's natural development and growth and you can see it in any group of young children. Very young children run in a very bouncy un-grounded way, with their legs flying all over the place. By the age of five to seven most run more smoothly as they start to feel more grounded for themselves. As you grow up, you need to develop and experience your own grounding.

Being born to grounded parents gives you an experience of grounding at a very young age. When you are born, you can ground through your parents who carry us about and we can continue to ground like this for some time. If your parents are very un-grounded, however, you may struggle to ever get that experience for yourself and hence will have much difficulty in developing it naturally. Grounding is a skill you can easily learn.

Children can imagine they are a tree, letting energy flow up into them and passing stuff they don't want, back down into the ground, to the centre of the earth. You can play with having just one tree or having one tree root connected to each foot. We often use this for adults too. I find an old fashioned egg timer invaluable. As you watch the sand pass through, you can gradually become more and more grounded. There are many metaphors or techniques you use to achieve this state, however. See what works best for you!

Grounding yourself is a natural process. For instance, to stand on one leg we have to ground through the other or we fall over. You can get grounded by walking without shoes in nature or doing something that requires focus. There are more convenient and empowering ways which, with practice, can be just as powerful. These can be used anywhere, at anytime.

Try this one for yourself; it only takes a few minutes. You can do it waiting in a queue, on your way to work, in an aeroplane or at school, without anyone knowing what you're doing.

✓ **Sit comfortably with both feet in contact with the floor, (you can remove your shoes if you prefer, or, even better, sit outside on the grass).**

✓ Become aware of your breath, noticing it without trying to control it. Relax and enjoy the sensation of your breath entering and leaving your body.

✓ Keeping the awareness of your breath, become aware of the soles of your feet and your connection with the floor. How do your feet feel on the ground? Energy follows thought, so by taking your attention to your feet, more blood will flow into your feet and you may feel them becoming warmer.

✓ When you can feel your feet and your attention is in your feet, imagine the centre of the earth beaming energy into the soles of your feet and that your inner spirit is controlling the flow of energy that is right for you. Notice how it feels as it swirls through, gently allowing the energy to clear and clean all the energy channels in your feet, your ankles, your calves, your knees, your thighs, your pelvis and collecting all of this at the base of your spine.

✓ Imagine accessing that pool of electrons that can flow through all those points on your feet and find just the right route to any free radicals in your body manifested as pain, stiffness, etc.

✓ Then allow the centre of the earth to send up a tube, your "grounding cord," to the base of your spine, wide enough for a football. Lock this onto the base of your spine. Consider for a moment that every cell in your body is a little light which has a matching light to every point in your energetic body. When you connect to your "grounding cord", imagine pulling your true essence down a little so all these pairs of lights match up. You may feel a drop of say half an inch in your body as you firmly connect your "grounding cord" to the base of your spine. If for some reason you have been very un-grounded, you may feel a much larger drop. Notice how that helps you feel "more like you."

✓ Enjoy that feeling of being firmly connected to the earth, with energy flowing up through your feet and down through the base of your spine.

✓ You can connect into this "grounding chord" any male or female energy that isn't yours. For example, you may be carrying around energy from your mother and father. You can also run little tubes from your male or female organs so that they can "let go" of excessive feelings of responsibility and nurturing in a regular, continuous and gentle way, all under the control of your spirit.

✓ If any thoughts or emotions arise, bring your attention back into your body and to this grounding loop of energy, to wash them away by just re-setting your intention.

✓ As you get more practised, you can extend this loop, bringing the energy up to your solar plexus just below your rib cage and then shining all the way down your spine. You can then choose to bring this energy further, into your chest, neck and head, each time dropping back down into your "grounding chord."

✓ You can run this for five minutes, ten minutes, fifteen minutes, or for as long as you want. Whatever you choose will benefit you.

✓ What have you noticed about the experience, how do you feel now?

There are many simple ways to ground – select what works for you. Here are a few additional tips:

• You will find sitting on the toilet is a very grounding place as the plumbing is connected deep into the ground, especially when your bathroom is on the ground floor.

• Try drinking water, this can really help, especially if you also take Omega-3 oil to keep water inside your cells, and increase your body's hydration.

• Avoid sugar, fizzy drinks, e-numbers, caffeine and chocolate.

• Try moving to a place away from electronic equipment and see what that feels like.

- Walking in bobbly socks or on uneven pebbles can help by stimulating the soles of your feet. You can see children naturally improving their gait as they walk on pebbles and become more grounded.

- It is very useful to anchor grounding into a physical activity like walking through a doorway or sitting in a chair. In this way, you gain an immediate trigger at various times in the day. You may find using your computer is very un-grounding, especially as it may trigger rapid responses from you; sitting at your computer is therefore a great place to anchor grounding. See yourself sitting down, grounding and notice what you feel – make sure your grounding goes right down into the centre of the earth and just relax into the chair. Rehearse it as often as you like until it becomes your natural state when using your computer.

- Imagine grabbing all those busy thoughts from your head, bringing them down into the area around your belly button[30] – and passing them down into the floor, into the centre of the earth.

- There are many complementary therapies like massage and reflexology that can help you to get grounded too.

Grounding foods tend to be those that have been cooked, and generally cooked for longer periods than an average meal. For example:

- Casseroles with whole brown rice and a protein.

- Porridge for breakfast or a smoothie with omega oils in it (which makes it slower releasing).
- Dahl and rice adding calming spices such as cinnamon and nutmeg.
- Fish or lean meat and vegetables.
- Roasted sweet potato with butter or with tuna fish.

For an emergency grounding, try a bowl of slow cooked oats or brown rice with rice milk and some flax oil. This can be very healing and calming to the body, mind and soul[31].

That said, a state of grounded-ness cannot be taken for granted. If you have difficulty with the grounding process, or find yourself dropping into negative emotions, you may have severely blocked energy. The next chapter will help you with this, however. You can run the processes in both this and the next chapter. In doing so, you will begin to clear blocks and becoming increasingly grounded. For maximum effect, you will need to continue clearing and grounding on a regular basis. As I have mentioned before, grounding is the personal hygiene for your energy system. Consider it a complement to your other personal maintenance chores, such as brushing your teeth and washing.

Changing States

Why is it you can sometimes concentrate and at other times feel "all over the place?" Why are some young people calm and peaceful at home, yet a nightmare in school, whilst others are withdrawn in school and a challenge at home?

Crucially, being grounded or un-grounded are not *permanent* states.

They fluctuate and they can be changed. In order to better understand your daily energy changes, it is worth taking the time to understand what causes you to become un-grounded and how you become grounded again. Try to start noticing how you feel and what is happening in your body. You may find you can be grounded one minute, yet un-grounded the next. These are clues to helping you achieve a more consistent, grounded state. If you are doing this with your child, help them to explain what is going on for them as they may not have the language to be able to tell you. You will find this gives you many insights.

There are many possible reasons for people's state to change on a daily basis. These might include:

- The frantic pace of modern life.

- Trauma and pain – not wanting to be in your body.
- Confusion – maybe feeling as if you aren't on the planet!
- Rapid thoughts of worry or frantic planning.
- Energy blocks that prevent grounding. These may be caused by past events, such as operations, injuries, limiting beliefs or significant negative emotions. This could very easily be central for those who are struggling at school.
- Picking up energy which disturbs your energy system; this could include other peoples' energy, that of your environment or of electrical equipment.
- Fizzy drinks, colourings, junk food, chocolate, sugar, e-numbers, caffeine and refined foods.

- Being over-excited.
- Being affected by others who are un-grounded.
- Being insulated from the ground by shoes, being in high buildings or walking on insulating materials.
- Living and sleeping in an un-grounded environment.

Moving beyond the question of why you are un-grounded, you can begin to consider a number of ways in which you might become better grounded. Consider for a moment the situations in which you feel your most relaxed, calm and focused.   This might include any of the following:

- Relaxing in a safe and comfortable environment.
- Taking a walk in the forest.
- Paddling in the sea.
- Being really in your body and noticing your experience.
- Being present (not worrying about the past or the future).
- Being in the presence of grounded people.
- Practise positive emotions such as gratitude, love or appreciation coming from your heart[32]
- Feeling valued and validated.
- Setting a clear intention to stay grounded.

In time, being un-grounded can progress to a learnt behaviour and a habit.   In time, this may manifest itself in health challenges and SpLDs. For example:

ADHD – An adult client, recently diagnosed with ADHD recently contacted me with a diagnosis of ADHD. He talked about all the normal symptoms. I asked him what was happening when he felt OK and what was happening when he felt confused? As we talked, I introduced the concept of grounding. I asked him to keep a diary for a week, noting what caused/triggered which state. After a week he reported this was the most useful advice he had ever been given and he wanted more time to really understand and develop these observations before he went any further.

Tourette's Syndrome – people describe the sensation of something building up internally, running up through their body until they have to shout to relieve the pressure. Teaching them to ground themselves and their environment can redirect the energy into the ground. The younger this is done, the easier it is to change the behaviour before it becomes an extended habit.

Asperger's Syndrome – A mother of a child with Asperger's picked up her child from school and noticed he was speaking in a very strange sort of Mickey Mouse voice. Remembering what she had learnt about grounding, she grounded herself next to him and immediately his voice returned to normal.

Dyslexia and Chronic Fatigue – Exhaustion is common with poor literacy and one young woman, who agreed she was never grounded, had, by the age of twenty-four, developed Chronic Fatigue as well. Poor literacy is indeed exhausting.

The Environment

Sometimes we find it difficult to ground ourselves in a chaotic environment, for example a noisy classroom, a messy work area or a crowded train. A classroom with lots of posters on the wall looks great, but too much external stimulus can overload a child. They become un-grounded and are unable to concentrate.

In addition, when a child gets upset and can't articulate the problem they are facing, they may well be un-grounded. Parents may then become stressed and un-grounded too. The child then picks up on the environment and their stress and "the balloon goes up!"

This chain of events can be seen in various different settings. For example, business meetings are a place where the environment can very quickly change from supportive to hostile. You can learn to calm the environment, helping those present make better decisions.

Simple skill #2: Grounding the Physical Environment

When there is a lot of activity in the environment around you, it helps you to ground yourself if you are first able to ground the environment. For example, when children first come into a classroom, there will be a lot of different energies circulating. To solve this problem, a child can settle these down by simply grounding the room. Having done so, the environment and those in it will be more productive.

Here is a simple process to assist you in setting the energy of the environment. To begin, take an easy deep breath into your tummy, without raising your shoulders; don't force it, just an easy deep breath.

✓ **Imagine gold energy and amethyst energy; that light purple colour of an amethyst crystal. Imagine that the ceiling and the walls of the room that you are in are filling up with gold and amethyst energy, coming from the universe. As it collects into a large ball of energy, anchor that right down to the centre of the earth and feel supported by the earth's energy.**

✓ **Notice how this feels in your body as the energy of the room settles down.**

Grounding the space can be invaluable for getting a class to settle down and focus. To ground a classroom, teachers can ask the children to imagine a big tree in the middle of the room (or in the middle of each table) with roots going right down into the centre of the earth. This effectively takes away all the energy you don't need in the classroom, helping to provide a calm environment for learning.

For Young Children

You can introduce any of the above processes to young children in a fun way through play, including having their own grounding when they go to school. Even the children's game of statues is a good way to get grounded as everyone has to stay very still.

Grounding is contagious. When you get yourself grounded, a child who is on your knee or you are carrying will energetically start to feel grounded too. This is often very helpful with a crying or distressed child. Do it slowly, noticing how it will helps them relax. As they grow up, teach them how to do it for themselves so they can use the skill anytime.

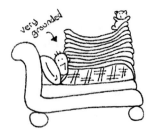

Many people crave to be grounded, especially those who get very stressed and can only do it physically by lying under heavy bedclothes, going for a massage, sitting close to a family member, walking on the beach or taking some physical exercise. There are products, such as weighted blankets that help people ground. For some people, a weighted blanket has instant results and is a great demonstration. Once you learn to ground, you will find you can do it anywhere, in seconds without the need for external assistance, and without anyone realising. Teaching people to ground through the power of their mind is a gift.

Chapter 9: What Holds You Back?

Working on being more grounded will give you insights as to where your energy is being blocked and potentially inform you about the reasons behind your being un-grounded in certain circumstances. In this chapter, you will learn simple ways to release these blocks; the central objective here is to let your energy flow easily through and around your body.

Blocks That Manifest as SpLDs

Those with SpLD manifest some of the following symptoms, which are often caused by energy blockages:

- Lack of core stability and poor co-ordination, e.g. Dyspraxia.
- Poor fine and gross motor skills.
- Low self esteem.
- Feeling physically blocked.
- Feeling exhausted.
- Confusion.

As you run the grounding processes described in the previous chapter, you may find things come up which seem to block your success or make you feel uncomfortable. When this happens try releasing the block and go back to the last chapter, swapping between the two until you are really firmly grounded. This chapter is designed to help you release anything that clogs you up and move on. By the end of the chapter you will find yourself much lighter, freer and more in contact with that bright shining being you really are.

For humans to function at their optimum capacity, energy must flow unimpeded through energy pathways, energising physical, emotional and mental aspects of the body. Look at your hands for a moment and consider what they would look like if you had never washed them. In a similar way, your energy system can get just as dirty. Several techniques are available to assist you with cleaning your energy, including Reflexology, Reiki, meditation and Energetic NLP, which is used extensively in this book. With Energetic NLP you use the power of thought to clear and enhance your energy channels, anywhere, anytime. You will find your thoughts are clearer and you can make better decisions.

This chapter will help you clear blocks to success, whether or not you have consciously identified them and give you motivation to change. Your energy flow can be blocked by accidents, operations, low self esteem, being sensitive to energy, negativity in your life and traumas (such as a traumatic birth or other negative experiences). In the following pages, you will learn how to release them through simple, guided imagery.

Creating Resilience

As a metaphor, consider for the moment the lifecycle of a spider's web, which starts as an intricate construction of perfection. Very quickly the web gets little things sticking to it. The energy of the web may not be quite the same as it was before, the perfect symmetry may have been broken and the air may not be able to circulate in quite the same way. Over time, these little clogs become larger, distorting the web and blocking the energy flow, attracting more and more stuff until part of the web starts to collapse. Soon it turns into a tangled mess that the spider can't fix and it is abandoned; all interest is gone. If an attentive spider had come along at an early stage, the web could have been repaired. The longer it's left, the harder it is to make positive changes, although – if truth be told – it is never too late!

We are born bright and sparkling into a new world of possibilities. Then things start to happen and we collect beliefs, programming from our parents, our schools, our friends and other sources as to what is and isn't possible, what is and isn't acceptable, etc., etc. Some of what we're taught shows us how to act safely and profitably within society. Other things we learn, however, may be limiting and hold us back. So our own personal spider's web may be holding ideas we have picked up from others that may contribute to us losing sight of the fabulous sparkling web we were born as. Alternatively, we may live in a nurturing environment of infinite possibilities and extraordinary potential. We may just be able to dust off negativity, stay connected to ourselves and learn from experiences without becoming clogged up with all the stuff surrounding those experiences. In short we become resilient to things that happen, feeding a "can do" attitude.

Motivation

In life, we do little without motivation. We are motivated by wanting something (the carrot), or being afraid of not doing it (the stick)! We can be motivated at one level (losing weight, stopping smoking), yet unmotivated at another because of beliefs, value etc. ("I can't give up", "it won't last", "who would I be"?). Once we are fully aligned towards a goal, progress is easier.

Motivating a child to make changes can, as every parent knows, be an interesting challenge; the change has to be something they really want to do. For example, a young person who is always wobbly (like a weeble toy) has learnt to accept that this is the way they are. They may decide they don't like sports. Is there some part of this they would like to change? For example, not tripping over in the playground, not being knocked over or bullied by bigger children? Teach your child to get grounded and release any blocks that are stopping them from doing so. Everyone has the right to be grounded. We live on the planet, needing to be "down to earth".

Simple Skill #3: Releasing to the Lake and the Magnet

Before discussing any more blocks that can arise, it is beneficial to learn a simply way of releasing things you no longer need or want, especially those identified earlier that are created when our learning process is not successful. You can immediately release anything that is ready to go. Just imagine anything that upsets you gently draining down into the ground, through those tree roots or your "grounding chord". Watching an egg-timer can be great for assisting with relaxation and letting you gently sink into a grounded state.

It is important that you don't skip this section, because you need to have the experience of clearing energy blocks before going into more detail about finding your own blocks and helping others release theirs.

For a more comprehensive release try this meditation; a core process called the "magnet in the lake" which will help you to "let go" of things that are holding you stuck. You can use it any time you are triggered by something or someone.

✓ Sit comfortably and quietly with your feet flat on the floor, arms and legs uncrossed and your back fairly straight. Settle down and get grounded, as above. Take two or three deep breaths, allowing all your muscles to relax, especially your jaw, chest, abdomen and feet.

✓ Each time you breathe in, breathe all the way down into your tummy and as you breathe out, feel all the muscles in your body relaxing. Set the intent that you can now "let go" of anything you no longer need and you will have taken any learning you need.

✓ Close your eyes and imagine a deep sea, lake, or river before you. Give the water whatever surroundings you like. Don't worry about whether you see it clearly, holographically, as a cartoon, in black and white or just sort of know it's there. Any of these will work very effectively.

✓ Imagine at the very deepest point in this water there is a magnet. This magnet is so powerful it can attract negative beliefs, programming, old emotions, karma, limiting beliefs that no longer fit, or other people's energy out of the cells in your body.

✓ Fix your attention on the magnet and imagine it is gently and powerfully pulling anything you no longer need out of your cells. Trust that your unconscious mind will only get rid of whatever is not of benefit or is not serving you. (Your unconscious is very conservative, so if it's willing to "let go", you can be sure it is safe to lose these things).

- ✓ Whilst the magnet is working, you may get images, or feelings, or you may hear sounds as things just leave you. Whatever your experience, this is right for you.
- ✓ Allow the magnet to pull out whatever form these energies take and suck them into the water, down into the centre of the earth for processing back into new healing and enhancing energies.
- ✓ Don't bother to analyse what is coming away – you may see little cartoons or simply hear or feel things leaving. As they go into the water, just let them dissolve.
- ✓ If you don't feel anything's happening, just imagine that you're removing whatever is blocking you.
- ✓ If it still seems blocked, remove whatever's blocking the block.
- ✓ If you're still not getting a sense of this working, remove the block that's blocking the block that's blocking the block!
- ✓ At this point, there will be nothing left to block anything.
- ✓ Now, let the magnet do its work.
- ✓ From time to time, you may like to scan your body from your feet right up to the crown of your head, making sure the magnet is dealing with every last residue.
- ✓ Imagine the magnet working for as long as you feel is appropriate, knowing you can turn the intensity up or down and stop whenever you like.
- ✓ When the magnet has finished its work, dispose of both the image and magnet. Some people like to explode it into millions of tiny pieces that fly out into space; some people send it down into the centre of the earth where it is reprocessed into positive energy; some people wrap it up and throw it in a metaphoric bin. Do whatever works for you.
- ✓ Now imagine a golden ball of positive healing energy hovering above you. Pay attention to the ball and imagine it growing and sparkling. Now, allow the golden energy to filter through your skin, filling any gaps that are left. Let any excess just go into the ground.

✓ Try and run this at least twice a day (on waking and prior to going to bed). In addition, use it any time you wish to remove energy that you may have picked up in a particular circumstance.

✓ If you are in the shower or the bath, you may make use of the water to imagine it cleaning and clearing your entire aura and energy system. You could even imagine a sacred lake or ocean where you swim, letting the water completely run through you.

As you read through this book, you may find things that trigger you. You can convert this into an extraordinary learning experience if you release your energy of resistance whenever this happens. That doesn't mean you are expected to agree with everything, but clearing the energy of your reaction will help you think clearly, be curious and let your own inner wisdom decide whether the content is right for you at this time.

For Young Children

This basic process can be altered to make it more helpful to young children. Sometimes I ask young people who are feeling bad about something or themselves what the fastest thing they can think of is. For some, this is perhaps a cheetah or a rocket ship. I ask them to fill it up with anything that is making them unhappy and send it off to the back of the moon. Then I suggest they find another, differently coloured one at the back of the moon and fill that with confidence. Bring it back and shower the confidence all over their head and body. In about a minute they have lost all the negativity that was blocking their progress. You can use anything that appeals to them, so long as it moves very fast. If you don't release all the energy in one go, just repeat the process; soon there will be nothing left to cause upset.

When the child has "let go" of something that was troubling them, get them to fill up with lovely golden energy so it doesn't come back. For young children, just thinking of filling up with sunshine is great.

Another example: for computer enthusiasts, the recycle bin on a computer screen is very useful. You can mentally fill it up with any stuff you don't want and then hit the empty button, even making the funny noise the computer makes. If you think it isn't working, imagine any blocks like a child's toy bricks and toss them in the recycle bin too.

Chapter 10: Building on Strengths

Having started to get your energy flowing well, it is time to look at the exceptional skills people have and see how they can be employed most effectively to overcome often debilitating symptoms. Most people with SpLD are also exceptionally talented, especially visually. This chapter is full of ways you can teach people to optimise and control their skills.

The Basics of Visual Learning

We are all born with the skill to retain visual images. How do we know this? A baby as young as six weeks will recognise their mother or another caring adult. Should that mum put on a funny wig, however, the child will almost certainly cry. The only way someone can have this recognition is to have a visual image of what the adult looks like. Even little things, like putting on a hat or make-up, can be enough to confuse a baby.

To understand visual learning, we have to put ourselves in the place of that child. Where do they hold their pictures? How bright are their pictures? How fast do they move? Once the child understands their own mental geography, they will have more control over their pictures. Visualising is fun; it's used effectively by many sports people (to visualise success) and with just a little introduction, everyone can find this skill invaluable.

This book focuses mainly on visual skills, as this is a common theme amongst those with SpLD. You will see how all our senses interrelate; visual (sight), auditory (hearing and internal dialogue), kinaesthetic (feelings), olfactory (smell), gustatory (taste); abbreviated VAKOG, plus others including our proprioception[33] sense (which signals to us where our body is in space), which is often inaccurate for those with an SpLD.

Every event in our lives is encoded into memory using a combination of these senses. Think about a happy event in your life and notice how you recall it. Do you get a visual, auditory, kinaesthetic, olfactory or gustatory memory first? Do the other senses then follow, and in what order do they do so? This is a simple example to enable you to check out your own experience, and it will give you some idea of how you personally code information and recall it.

The Sensory Mixing Desk

"The sensory mixing desk" (Figure 1) is a model to help you understand your own experience. Through the metaphor, you can view your senses as if on sliders, like an audio mixing desk with base, treble, and so on.

In my experience, people without SpLD have quite even senses and moment to moment flexibility. For example, when someone is engrossed in the television, an electronic game or reading the newspaper, they will have high visual and low auditory, to the point of appearing to be deaf. When they have finished, their hearing will revert to normal. Take the instance of someone who has lost their sight, they may actually gain improved hearing externally and internally to recall things they have heard previously. Dame Evelyn Glennie[34], a world famous percussionist, is nearly totally deaf, but can feel the music through her body.

Those with SpLD tend have more *extreme* sensory variations, however. They are often very visual (almost off the scale in some instances), but at the same time they can be very low or over-sensitive in auditory terms. In addition, they are likely to be very low kinaesthetically or oversensitive. My work has shown that once you start talking to children about their internal pictures and visual imagination – which is often their specialist subject – other senses may start to balance out.

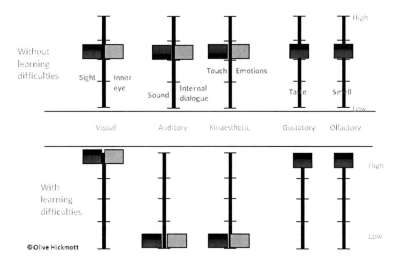

This basic pattern is regularly validated in individuals, in a variety of different ways. For example, children might have:

- Very high visual creative skills, recalling from visual memory and making new images in their imagination. Those higher up the autistic spectrum may have problems with imagination while having extraordinary recall. Great visual skills often run in families.

- A low ability to listen, especially to the sounds of words (the essential skills for learning phonics). Some may have had glue ear or grommets when they were young and those I work with, who are profoundly deaf, offer an extreme example of how the lack of one sense often results in the development of other senses. Visualisation is very easy for them, whilst phonics is very hard.
- Low kinaesthetic skills to the point of not exhibiting feelings and, at the same time, getting very emotional about what, to others, appear to be trivial matters.
- Either a lack of speech or an inability to stop talking about a favourite topic.
- An excellent ability to visualise in their mind's eye, even when only partially sighted. To each internal sense there is a matching external one, where, for example, your external eye shares much neurology with your mind's eye.
- Very good visual skills when playing on a computer and appearing nearly deaf, whereas normally they have perfect hearing. Note that standard tests for preferred learning styles don't take into account context.

The following stories will provide you with further insights into how learning visually interacts with other senses.

Whilst driving the car, I was listening to Alice in Wonderland on the radio and creating mental images of the story, the essential skill for comprehension. Near my destination I had to look at the map and concentrate on the road. The story kept playing but I had no idea at all about what happened in the story. My ears were switched off while concentrating on the map – another visual skill. How often do you read a book and your mind wanders off to more interesting things?

One of our trainers is a Radio4 addict who listens constantly in the car. She commonly has this same experience whenever she needs to turn her attention to more demanding road conditions. Her ears simply switch off as in my experience above. Conversely, when she is able to listen more easily whilst driving and hears something of particular interest, if she subsequently (perhaps a few days later) relates what she has heard to a third party, she usually get a visual flash of exactly where she was driving when she heard this information!

Mary said she had a real problem with short term memory, she just couldn't remember what she read. I started to read her the story of the Wizard of Oz. I read for about 30 seconds and asked her what the story was about. Her answer was shoes. Shoes was the last word I had said and, although she was familiar with the story, she was unable to recall any of it. Mary was in her feelings of "this is going to be impossible" and therefore blanking any visualising. So I suggested she made up pictures for every sentence and then run them like a movie. I read one sentence; she then told me about her pictures. I read the next; she summarised both and so on, until she could repeat the whole story. Mary had a fabulous visual memory and was studying Art, Photography and Media studies, but no-one had taught her how to convert the spoken word to pictures – the simple key to remembering what she read. Realising that was what was needed, she started with talking stories and then, as her reading improved, she could read and make up pictures at the same time. Many young people are labelled as having poor short term memory. With a little skills training, they may be able to change this dramatically.

A Little Bit of Brain Science

Visualising is a powerful and fun sport. It happens in the occipito-temporal region of your brain[35], roughly the place just beneath the crown of your head (where most people's hair changes direction). This is where you hold your pictures; if, for instance, I were to say to

you "see an elephant," you will have gone to that part of your brain and accessed a picture of an elephant. Even if I say "don't see an elephant," you will have gone to that same part of your brain, seen the picture while simultaneously trying to delete it. This all happens, of course, in a fraction of a second, out of your conscious awareness.

Now if I ask you to create a picture of a "lizard with green scales, wings and a forked tongue" you may go to your library of lizards, green scales, wings and forked tongues and start assembling this imaginary reptile. Alternatively you may be overwhelmed by too much information, too many unknowns and give up. You may have noticed this in those you are in contact with. Show this same person an image of the creature and they will have no problem recalling it later.

Once you understand more about visualising, you will be able to teach almost anything visually. It is not about showing people pictures; that is visual *teaching*. Visual *learning* is about you creating your own pictures from words, ideas and feelings to aid your memory. You don't need to be a great artist, as these are pictures you keep in your head for your use. If you are good at art you may like to put some on paper, but that's certainly not essential. For example, when listening to a story, everyone will make up different pictures. This is perfect, a habit that should be encouraged and the essence of creativity.

Symptoms of Unbalanced Sensory Systems

People have a whole range of experiences, most of which they have been doing for so long that they have become unconscious habits. It is useful to be able to recognise, in yourself or someone else, an unbalanced sensory system which is likely to appear as SpLDs. This issue might manifest in one or a few of the following symptoms:

- Inability to keep visual images still. Fast moving pictures out of control. Stress causes pictures to move even faster – some, so fast they appear only as black and white fog, as if on a badly tuned TV. When children run away they may be running away from themselves and this confusion.

- Totally engaged in your own visual world – resenting interruption (like being woken up in the middle of a good dream); zoning out, staring into nothingness, smiling at random; asking people to repeat what they have said; feeling overwhelmed by visual stimuli such as people's faces.

- Pictures which trigger negative emotions.

- Pictures in places which are inconvenient.

- Disinterest in reading and academic work.

- Massive confusion in thought organisation, tiredness.

- Poor short term memory.

Simple skills #4: Getting Your Visual Skills under Control

We visualise through our mind's eye and it is useful to be in control of these pictures, rather than have them controlling us. If you want to change your experience, go through the following steps and notice the changes in your mental geography. Several metaphors are included as examples; feel free to make up your own. Metaphors are great ways to communicate with your mind's eye:

- ✓ **Sit comfortably and quietly with your feet flat on the floor**
- ✓ **Find that grounded state and set up a magnet and a lake, (simple skills #1 and #3) to release any emotions that come up**
- ✓ **First look straight ahead and then raise your eyes to the ceiling, for 10 seconds, then come down again. If you have any discomfort, it is just the muscles in your eyes that are not exercised, so from time to time during the day look up for a few seconds and then come down again. Do this until you can manage it without any discomfort, then progress to the next step.**
- ✓ **Creating focus: Fix your eyes on a spot or dot about 30 degrees above eye level. Whilst looking at the spot, you will also be able to see objects around you in your peripheral vision. Expand your peripheral vision as far as you can, whilst maintaining focus on the spot and retain it for 20-30 breaths.**
- ✓ **Create a picture: Recall a picture of something with which you are familiar – perhaps a dog. (If you have any trouble visualising go to Appendix A and allow yourself time for a little basic practice). Some people visualise full colour images, some black and white, some have cartoons. With a little practice your images will improve. Don't forget that those with SpLDs normally have great pictures.**

✓ Motion and duration: Notice whether the dog is still or moving. Notice how long you can hold an image still. For some people it is just a flash for others it may be 10 minutes or longer. If it is just  a flash, you may want to ask yourself to see just one image for longer. The human brain can create still pictures or movies[36]. If yours are moving, get more grounded and just imagine that you can take a photograph, freeze frame it and create a still image. If you are used to playing electronic games or watching very fast movies, you may need to slow things down a lot and practise with grounding and a familiar situation, like cars stopping at red lights.

✓ Focus on one image: Just look at the image of a dog and switch off any other images that come to mind. Imagine tuning in the screen of a TV to get the best possible picture as follows:

✓ Location: Check where your image is. Too close to your face will be overwhelming, too far away or all around you will not be easy. Adjust the image to be about three to five feet (one to two metres) away and slightly up from your eye line. Notice whether it is clearer on the left or the right. Straight ahead is not advisable, as you may lose parts of the image as you switch from left eye dominance to right eye dominance. Your image may even be in your peripheral vision. Are you looking through your own eyes or are you using a different perceptual position – do you feel as if you are looking through your forehead? Notice which works best for you.

✓ Size: Notice how large or small the image is. If you want to adjust the size, think of what you would do on a computer to just drag the corner of an image to resize it. In just the same way you can re-size your image.

✓ **You may also like to give your screen an imaginary clean from time to time.**

Now you are starting to gain control over your pictures, you will need practice. Find what is right for you and notice as you make conscious changes: try to understand how this affects you. Many individuals will express a feeling of relief that they are back in control of what is happening to them, remarking that they didn't know it was so easy. Few people enjoy being out of control, for it is often a scary experience. If you already have this control, try noticing/imagining what your experience would be if you didn't have it.

When visualisation skills surpass a young person's artistic or written abilities, you can only find out by asking them what they are seeing. One of the challenges for teachers is that when they can't see a young person's pictures, there's nothing tangible for the teacher to grade or assess. You may be amazed just how creative the young mind is! To gain some information, watch the position and focus of the child's eyes. If they are looking up they will be accessing their pictures. You may even be able to gather from their eye movement whether they are seeing still or moving pictures. If they look sideways[37], they will be accessing sounds, whilst looking down helps them access emotions and their internal dialogue. Let the individuals decide whether left or right is better for recalling information and constructing new information.

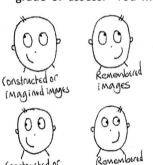

Constructed or imagined images

Remembered images

Constructed or imagined sounds

Remembered sounds

Feelings

Self-talk

Just take a little time to observe. If they seem to be in a trance, they will probably be really enjoying some movie, in which they themselves may be acting. You often see young people smiling in a way you perceive as random; however it isn't random to them, as they are fully engaged in their story which is entertaining to them. We call this day-dreaming; it can be very enjoyable for the daydreamer, but frustrating to others who are trying to get such people to focus on particular tasks. However, in this state the individual may be doing some very important stuff, be in full flow of concentration and dislike being interrupted. You won't know what is going on for them unless you ask them a question.

If the pictures in your mind's eye are scary, it is important to remember they are only pictures. Looking up will immediately reduce any emotion. You can then push any unpleasant pictures far enough away to allow you to relax. Think of something you like and at the same time make the bad picture smaller and the good picture larger. You can use this to help a small child who sees monsters. Alternatively, teach the child that when they see a monster (perhaps when they are 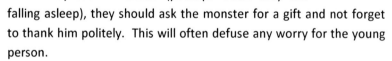 falling asleep), they should ask the monster for a gift and not forget to thank him politely. This will often defuse any worry for the young person.

Chapter 11: Learning as a Family

Our families and extended families are at the centre of the learning process. This can give rise to both positive and negatives. We may well find that young people are mirroring behaviours, at some level of family members. When the whole family engages in learning, it stops passing the challenges on to another generation. Our children can teach us much and when we learn as a family the benefits to all are clear.

Family Learning

This chapter focuses on the whole *system* that surrounds an individual with SpLD. By "system," I mean the set of social relationships – be they familial – such as parents, siblings, uncles, aunts, grandparents and other extended family members - or communal – such as teachers, school administrators and friends – that the child is a part of. We will look at how that individual affects the system around them, and how the system around them in turn affects the individual.

Have you ever put your glasses on the top of your head, and then desperately tried to find them? Other people can easily see the solution, and you have no idea. One of the extraordinary things I have clearly seen in families is children manifesting the  behaviours of their parents, although perhaps in a different way. Could this be a child's attempt to help the parent, showing what is obvious on the outside and not on the inside? Could it be glorified self interest to share a burden, in order to keep their parents healthy, so they can look after them? Young people often mirror the parent's challenges or those of someone else in their extended family system. As such, it may be easier for parents to understand their own problems when they see someone else manifesting them. Of course, this will often press the parents' buttons[38], generating even more stress, although the young person is unlikely to be consciously trying to achieve this.

I meet so many parents who volunteer statements such as: "I have learnt so much from this experience", or "I can see in my son all the traits I have struggled with", or "I would never have learnt to read if it hadn't been for my son". Personally, I would never have gained the confidence to read aloud if it hadn't been for the opportunity to read to my son as a baby without the risk of criticism.

The downside of this is that people so often jump to the intellectual conclusion that issues associated with SpLD must be genetic. The first time I saw a child overcome Dyslexia in a special needs school, I knew that all the confusion with words couldn't be genetic – it was simply a matter of time and effort that would allow children to shift their patterns, along with those of their families. Making things trickier, parents may be reluctant to do anything to help themselves, as they may have to face their deepest fears. Paradoxically, however, these same people will do anything to avoid their child having to struggle with the same challenges as they have had to deal with.

At different levels, parents can achieve profound change in themselves while at the same time helping their children. We are all familiar with one child copying another's temper tantrums. This reflective behaviour can be seen, to varying degrees, from anyone within the family system. Indeed, one person in a family can create significant shifts in a whole group. The system may include parents, siblings, friends, other relatives, their whole ancestral line, school teachers, learning assistants and even whole communities. The system as a whole will not change without motivation, and this process may be triggered as a result of helping just one individual initially. To me, the whole process of addressing SpLDs is about people learning together from the experiences around them and taking that learning forward into their everyday lives. This is family learning in the broadest possible sense.

Genetics May Not be as Important as People Think

Simply put, genetics is one of the most damaging beliefs currently circulating in conversations about health and SpLDs. We believe we can't do something because it isn't in our genetic make-up. Even though people like Bruce Lipton, a respected scientist, are beginning to prove our DNA is changeable[39], the general perception is that a genetic condition is something that has to be lived with. Fundamentally, this reduces people's sense of empowerment and convinces them that they are unable to change or address their SpLD.

Putting that aside for the moment, let's assume that none of these SpLDs are genetic; they may just be behaviours that you see running in families. That will immediately free your mind to consider other possibilities and all sorts of opportunities will open up. So, just for a minute, consider how things would be if there was no perceived genetic link. We would stop blaming our parents; we would see past the problems and could start learning as a family unit in a healthier, less blame-oriented manner. We would begin to understand that although family members do often have similar challenges, they are not the sole cause of SpLD issues. Visual people are talented and creative. With a landscape gardener father and a graphic designer mother, you are more than likely to have great visual skills, whether nature or nurture.

I was once told by a member of a Dyslexia charity not to give people false hope, as Dyslexia was a genetic disease. In my experience, getting other family members engaged turns around this link into something that is in fact very positive. Moving away from a pattern of blame, families can start to believe that they can all work together to address and solve the issues they face.

Huge sums are being spent on genetic projects around the world. Such projects are producing some valuable work, but they are also keeping our beliefs stuck in the same rut. For most people, finding a gene means laying the blame on parents and adopting a firm conviction that nothing can be done to make changes. According to research, however, genes can in fact change and differences can be caused by the environment.

This leads to my empowering approach through the belief that those who engage in this approach can achieve anything. The more we collaborate and share our experiences, the better the world will be. Just believing in someone's abilities will have a positive outcome[40].

The following story gives an example of the "dance" that changing experiences with various family members can bring about:

Jim and Jamie's story - Family learning is vital

Feb 2010 in Mum's words: "My partner, Jim was assessed and diagnosed as Dyslexic in his last year at secondary school. Jamie, my daughter (nine years old), was never diagnosed although her symptoms were identical to Jim's. She hated school. I pushed for the school to recognise her dyslexia, but they always said she could not be assessed as she wasn't one of the worst in the school and the money allocated for assessments was spent on the children with the worst problems. She was offered extra reading one to one. So I found help outside of school, as I felt extra reading was only going to add to her frustration and not help with the problem. I knew my daughter was very visual and brilliant at pictures".

Appointment with Olive: Jim and Jamie learnt how to visualise words and hold words still. The more Jim joined in, the more enthusiastic Jamie became. They also learnt to check, when they were reading, for the most comfortable position - nearly always holding the book up and not looking down on the words, to avoid negative emotions. Jim had one particularly startling response. He was looking at a book with pictures on one page and words on the opposite page. He just couldn't keep his eyes on the words when looking down. His eyes automatically crossed to the page with pictures. But when he held the book up, he reported "there are words on the paper" and started to read.

Four days later: "When I sent my partner and daughter off to see Olive for a coaching session, I expected them to come home with some new skills to help them improve their reading and spelling. I was not prepared to be totally amazed at the results.

My partner, who I've known for twelve years, has never read a book or willingly helped our children with homework as he found it too frustrating. Since his appointment he has sat at the table writing, spelling and reading with our children. He has also been teaching our six year old (who was starting to show signs of dyslexia) the skills he had learnt from Olive. I truly am blown away with how his confidence has grown, and he is motivated, encouraging and teaching our children all his new skills.

Our daughter, who would protest as soon as we started doing spellings or reading, is now excited and can whizz through learning new words. She is even spelling them backwards! Not only has this made a difference to them both individually and it has also improved our family life.

The stress levels in the house have gone right down, confidence has grown, there is more co-operation and some very happy people. I believe the skills taught by Empowering Learning[41] are a must for schools. If my partner had been taught this information in school, his whole school life could have been different. He would have left school with good grades and a sense of achievement, instead of being a "problem kid" and leaving school feeling a failure.

Our daughter has been lucky to learn this at the age of nine and will now have the opportunity to succeed in school. Teaching this in schools would have a massive positive impact. If children read and write, they are happier more confident motivated kids and therefore teachers' jobs would be easier, grades would go up. Money savings would be made as extra staff wouldn't need to come in. I would love to see schools benefit as much as our family has".

After four weeks: "I have found that Jamie is practising on her own when a new word comes up, or with Jim. I think I can get a bit over-enthusiastic and she gets fed up with that!!! When I used to work with Jamie, it felt as if every day we were starting over from scratch. Now it feels like she is making progress each day. Her reading has become more fluent as she isn't stopping at every word. She is finding it easier and faster to sound words out too. Jim said he feels so much more relaxed now around literacy as he feels he has a tool he can use anytime, anywhere. He is also reading with the kids more and I haven't got him asking me over and over how to spell the same word. He is also reminding the kids to look up and he has been practising with Jamie.

My six year old is using the white board very well to learn her spellings, and is so pleased when she can spell the words backwards! I have learnt that I need to be much more patient with them and things go better when they are working at their own pace. I told the school about Jamie and Jim seeing Olive. I also gave the school the book and web site details. My personal feeling was that they didn't seem to be interested, or it could be that they are just too busy with paperwork!"

After three months: Jamie's progress has been slow and I found that when I backed off and concentrated on Laurie (my six year old daughter), Jamie saw the progress Laurie made and is now much more willing to put in the effort.

Laurie can now learn seven spellings in one evening and she remembers them. For the past seven weeks she has got full marks in every spelling test at school. Previously she would have only learnt one per evening and would not have remembered them all for the test. Her reading flows much more now too. Jamie has gone up a reading level and has been told she will probably be moving up another level soon. Jim is still using the techniques and his confidence continues to grow.

After ten months: "Life is good in our household. Jamie is working towards her SATS at the moment. She is reading every day without me nagging! She also asked for books for Christmas!!!! There is no battle with her any more over homework and she is much more confident with her literacy work, even though it's not her favourite subject!

Jim said he loves the white board as he knows now that if he wants to learn a word, he speaks it into his phone, the phone spells it for him and he puts it on his imaginary white board. I suppose life is a whole lot easier, for all of us!

It seems amazing now that in one appointment so much was achieved - it just set them on a path of learning that they had never realised could be so valuable. They had to do the practice and the difference has been extraordinary".

SpLDs Can Be a Health Hazard

Many SpLDs can be a health hazard for the individual and the wider system. It is evident in Jim and Jamie's story, the reduction in stress levels was dramatic. If you add to this improved grounding and the calm it brings, the release of negative emotions, greater control, less anger and less confusion – you soon see benefits both physical and mental in both the long and short term. Further motivation for change is provided by the long list of adverse long term symptoms which people have reported, linked to a lifetime of SpLDs, which include:

- Increased blood pressure as a result of always being un-grounded and stressed.
- Accidents, due to feeling wobbly or having little internal safety dialogue.
- Dysfunctional and separated families.
- Regular exhaustion turning into Chronic Fatigue or ME for the individual and/or their family.
- Exhaustion from doing academic work with dyslexia; because of the constant use of the wrong part of the brain.

- Energy blocks experienced with several of the SpLDs, especially Dyspraxia, causing secondary problems as children grow, such as physical hip and knee problems.

The object of listing these examples is not to suggest that everyone will suffer them, but rather to encourage prevention and stop them occurring in the first place.

Simple Skill #5: Recovering Your Energy

One of the most important skills we learn from Energetic NLP is the ability to run our own energy. As we go through life, we pick up energies from other people. You will all be familiar with the following scenarios:

You have a friend who comes to see you when they are not in a good place. They may be fed up or tired and want a "shoulder to cry on". When they have finished telling you how awful life is, how do they feel? How do you feel? They probably feel much better, which is why they came to see you. On the other hand, you probably feel a whole lot worse, having quite literally "picked up their stuff". Now that you are running their stuff, when you interact with someone else, are you responding as you or as your friend?

John was nine years old and highly intelligent. He had always struggled with reading. He would instantly become ungrounded, his face would start to pucker up, his voice would start to tremble and he lost all sense of what he was reading. I taught him to ground all those negative emotions and every time he felt it growing he was to stop reading and release it into his roots.

We lose our energy through stress, poor diet, not enough sleep, not enough exercise, holding our breath, over responsibility, procrastination, overwhelm, fear, etc.

In families, you can easily pick up other people's energy without noticing. For example, what do you feel like when you wear someone else's coat? If you are very close to that person it may feel alright, but if they are not such a close connection it can feel very uncomfortable. You are picking up their energy and it is not right for you.

As such, the central question must be: When you see the same traits in several family members, are you seeing something handed down through genetics, or just the energy of someone else's behaviour? It is interesting to note that the National Autistic Society (NAS) in the UK, talk about various behaviours of Autism, and we all know behaviours can be changed if an individual wants to and they know **how to**, at every level of their being and in every part of their existence.

> Someone was helping me with a simple task one day, when they started to moan about people I knew. By the end of the day I found myself joining in the moaning and it was still happening after they had left. Moaning about others really isn't like me. I had picked up "the moaning energy"! As soon as I realised this, I didn't get into judgement about the person that would have given the energy more power. I simply sent it straight into the lake via the magnet. I then felt a lot more like me.

This is a simple way to release family energies and help you re-connect to your own energy. Set the intent; you want your own energy back whilst other family members will find their own energy better for them than yours.

- ✓ Sit comfortably with your feet flat on the floor, arms and legs uncrossed.
- ✓ Take two or three deep breaths and allow your muscles to relax.
- ✓ Close your eyes and imagine a golden ball of energy above your head.
- ✓ Pay attention to the golden ball and allow the ball to retrieve your energy from wherever you may have left it – in different places, with various people, in your dreams, on holiday, etc.
- ✓ Being on the planet, you need and have the right to have all your own energy with you, wherever you have deliberately or accidently left it. The planet is your home, you can bring all your energy to you.
- ✓ If you notice any resistance from family members, imagine that family member and introduce them to energy from the earth and universal energy. Don't force it on them, just imagine giving it as a present with full permission for the person to ignore it if they choose.
- ✓ You have the right to all of your energy so imagine a golden ball above your head, allow it to retrieve your energy from this family member, knowing that they will have access to other energies which will be better for them to metabolise than your energy.
- ✓ If you hear, feel or see things shifting, this is great. If you don't, just imagine it will be happening anyway.
- ✓ Imagine the ball is retrieving your energy, you don't need any more conscious thought about what or how this is happening.
- ✓ When you feel you have finished for the moment, imagine the golden ball cleaning up your energy, charging it up and only beaming your real energy back into your body to revitalize you; allowing any other energy to go down into the ground.
- ✓ When it is complete, dissolve the images, some people send them into the earth for recycling, others make up their own metaphors.

✓ To do this for other family members you will need to get their permission or for children make it into a game.

Simple Skill #6: Your Own Grounding

Within families, young children often ground through their parents, especially their mother. It is part of a parents' responsibility for the family. As children grow, they learn to ground for themselves and should be encouraged in this independence (particularly around the time they go to school), so they can all have their own energy.

✓ Imagine you can dissolve your old grounding chord. Create a new grounding chord with today's date and time. This grounding chord is just for you. Ensure your grounding chord is clear of anyone else trying to use it. Make it good and wide to allow free flow of energy from you into the ground and from the centre of the earth into your energy system.

Whenever you create change in your energy system, recreate a new grounding chord in the present date and time and create an imaginary e-mail to send out to everyone, so they can still find you.

Looking at Parents of Young People with SpLD

I look at the skills of the parents. Parents may have the same exceptional visual skills as their children. However, they may have none of the debilitating symptoms, or they may have the symptoms and have managed to achieve the resilience to be successful anyway. I often meet two very visual parents with two very different children; one child is flying through school whilst the other is struggling. Understanding these family connections, you may now be able to see how people conclude that SpLDs are genetic, whereas it is probably the visual skills that are handed down, maybe nature or nurture.

Schools also find themselves in a difficult situation, as they can often see the traits of the child in parents, but are not able to offer any assistance as this would cross a very clear boundary in the schools' responsibilities. As an independent practitioner, however, I have the opportunity to choose to work with whole families whenever possible.

Let's not forget that these people are very talented. So what happens to them as they grow up and face various challenges and how do these challenges affect and manifest in their life?

Adults with SpLDs may be very successful in their chosen field. They are most commonly found in careers where the need for written words is secondary (although their restrictions may still hold them back):

- The caring professions: nursing, community workers, the emergency services.
- Building and manual trades: brick layers, carpenters, double glazing engineers, plumbers, construction workers.
- Retail: fast food service personnel, DIY store staff.
- The visual professions: artists, hair stylists.
- Technical visual professions: surveyors, architects, engineers, draughtsmen.
- Those with different perspectives: entrepreneurs, creatives, CEOs, (Chief Executives frequently show that they have a great capability for seeing a different perspective on a particular issue. When they use that same skill on words they are likely to have Dyslexic tendencies).

- The criminal/justice system: prison guards, (n.b. over 80% of offenders have Dyslexia, which of course doesn't help their rehabilitation).

People who are **hyperactive** and able to concentrate on several things at once are often found in careers calling for multitasking such as Sports Reporters or Web-designers.

People with great **verbal skills** will be found in public service work or the media.

Those with exceptional and very **rare creative skills** will be recognised in the creative arts: artists, screenplay writers. In addition, creative skills are invaluable in many other areas where it is important to be able to see problems from different perspectives, for example, in engineering or running a company.

Those who are more **disconnected** from the world can be found to be very successful working with animals or in the research world.

> Talking with a police sergeant one morning at a networking breakfast, He told me that he couldn't spell very well but he could always remember number plates. He went on to explain that when Headquarters called him on the radio and ask him to look for a specific car he didn't have a chance to write it down so just memorised a number plate. Five minutes later he was visualising words, using exactly the same skill. He could see all the words he wanted on number plates.

Mary's youngest son Robert (ten years old) was diagnosed with Asperger's and Sensory Processing Disorder. She is an NLP Master Practitioner and, while talking with Olive at a conference, mentioned some of the symptoms she was observing – Robert had difficulty interacting with people with the obvious symptom being his two voices, one normal, the other like Mickey Mouse. Robert swapped between them seamlessly. He was quite relaxed at home and had many more difficulties at school in a busy classroom. His spelling and reading were poor with visualising being on the periphery of his vision, making it difficult to see words. Once he got grounded and took control of the position of his pictures, he could visualise whole sentences!

William, Mary's older Son, (twenty three years old) had in Mary's word, "seemed to have learnt Dyslexia around the age of six" and this needed further exploration. When he started at school, he could clearly read - he was finishing one Biff and Chip book per night. But quite soon and after a few stressful incidents, Mary could clearly see his work deteriorating; she believes at that stage he was learning Dyslexia. He can recall having pictures all around him and only about six inches from his head – he now realises he was literally overwhelmed by them.

He is currently an estate agent, writing details of houses, which enable clients to conjure up pictures of the property - he is painting is a picture in words. At work, when using the computer, he is aware feeling very grounded.

Olive described a symptom of children visualising small words well, and, as the words become longer, losing the beginning, end, top and bottom of the word – as if looking at a cut-out of just the centre of the word. This immediately resonated with William because, when the words were all around him, that is exactly what he remembered seeing. As an adult, this had slowly corrected and now he could simply make sure the word was far enough away to capture it all. With this insight and after checking out the ideal position for him to hold a book, his reading is improving. Like many highly visual individuals, he was excellent at building Lego without the instructions and even building a whole city one time. He can take anything apart and put it back together again; he just retains the blueprint in his head – a fabulous visual skill.

Whilst helping her children, Mary has learnt so much and gained so many insights for herself. As she says, "We can all see Asperger's tendencies in ourselves", the only difference is that we aren't stuck in them. Working with Olive on grounding has helped her feel much more solid and cleared some old energy, that wasn't even her own. She can now feel energy running throughout her body, especially her legs, recalling the feeling from when she was young – a sensation which she loves.

Chapter 12: What Have You Learnt So Far?

You will have learnt about improving grounding, clearing blocks, rebalancing your sensory system and how aspects of SpLD are reflected through families. Your perspective of children with SpLD issues and their exceptional talents will be changing as you try out these tools.

I should also like to pass on to you some advice received when working in collaboration with Dr. Cheri Florance. I have often thought of these words when challenged by some of the unique symptoms a young person manifests: "When you have a skill that you know works in a particular situation, try using it in another when you are stuck and then deal with what is left. Your high frequency, easy to use skills, when paired with new emerging skills, will actually help the new skills stabilise. When you isolate the skill that is easiest to do or easiest to learn, focus on it aggressively and you can see how much improvement can be made. At this point re-evaluate and work on what is left.[42]" For example, my first Asperger's client couldn't spell so I taught them to spell visually and then several symptoms just vanished.

Support for You

The skills that you have learnt will not only help those with SpLD, but also help your own understanding and your experience. Grounding and clearing blocks are particularly useful for those who care for others with SpLD, enabling you can take better care of yourselves and cope with challenging situations.

Trying to help others and living with the daily challenges is, as everyone knows, very draining. It is important to realise, however, that for you to be of assistance, you also need to conserve your own energy. Letting go of anything that triggers you whenever you have a challenge will not only help you, but also help others. Naturally, this is easier said than done, but with practice it will become much easier. It is like the oxygen mask in an aeroplane – you need to look after yourself first; once you have achieved this, you will be available to help others more effectively.

I suggest you review Part 2 and write yourself some notes about changes you have noticed yourself and in other family members. Keeping a record of your progress (in a diary, for instance) will give you a real sense of achievement.

To reach this point you will have made progress and I should like to introduce the concept of validation for yourself and those you are helping. Whilst you are reviewing what you have learnt and put into practice, a little validation for everyone's achievements will accelerate further progress.

Simple Skill #7: Validation

Giving and receiving praise is something with which people often struggle. It would seem to be the easiest thing in the world but people who may often have no trouble giving praise are in fact very bad at receiving it. To use a helpful metaphor, imagine your "giving" and your "receiving" bowls; notice their size and adjust them to suit you.

Whenever you give praise, try to make it specific so it really resonates with the person. Saying your child is "great" will probably pass them by, as most of the time they feel anything but great. Telling them you really like the picture they have drawn, and why you like it,

will have far more impact and add to a young person's self-concept.

Validation is important for every living thing and is fundamental to achieving higher levels of grounding. For example, validation is central to your identity, beliefs and values. Just telling a child you love them (even if they are sleeping) will build their self esteem. If you feel blocked giving or receiving validation, picture this as wooden blocks which you can quite happily toss into the waste bin, send to the moon or any other metaphor you choose. If you would like some help to understand validation there is a fable on You Tube about the magic of free parking[43]. Having won many awards and millions of viewings, it easily demonstrates validation and you'll see how it can change your close relationships and those with the wider world. When, for example, a child or a parent has been through a traumatic birth, validating them for just being here may be all they need to help them feel more grounded.

✓ **Let me invite you to validate and acknowledge yourself for who you are and what you have achieved in your life to date.**

✓ **First just imagine a symbol that represents this and fill it up with all the unique ways you would like to be validated and acknowledged.**

✓ **When it is full enough, just open yourself up to receiving that validation and acknowledgement and taking it with you throughout your life.**

✓ **Notice how this feels for you.**

Now imagine that you can just ask someone else to produce a symbol for how they would like to be validated. Watch it fill up with energies from the earth and the universe about how they would like to be validated and invite the person to receive all that validation.

Making Progress with Other Family Members

Some of the skills you have learnt in this part of the book will be invaluable for many with SpLD, especially the overlap between Dyslexia, ADHD and Dyspraxia. Each one of these skills you will find is valuable to those you work with; after all, they are simply new skills that anyone can use. You can't do any harm helping people understand more about their own experience and how to change it. Just use whatever process seems most appropriate, learn from your own experience and remember to see the world through your children's very visual eyes – you will learn so much by asking them to explain their experiences.

PART 3:
ADVANCED SKILLS

Chapter 13: The Visual Elements of Literacy

Those who are good at literacy have the skill to see words in their mind's eye. If this is you, imagine what it would be like if you didn't have this skill. Not having this skill is the experience of many of our young people. It is, however, a simple skill to teach and develop. Everyone can do it. 100% of those I assist to learn visually had no concept that they needed to visualise still words, nor did they have any idea how to do it. Once they learnt this skill, they rapidly improved their literacy.

Being Good at Literacy

People who are good at spelling and reading look up, "see" words and can then write them down; this has been known for many years[44] and is confirmed by every good speller I meet. Phonics – a purely auditory technique – has been taught for several years, yet if young people were taught to visualise words at the same time, with the skills in this chapter, their experience of learning would be so much easier. Phonics is essential for any new word and once a child has come across a word two or three times it should move to their visual memory. We can even create the feeling of the word being correct and knowing what it sounds like – making literacy a synthesis of all our senses. If young people only use auditory senses, however, they will never achieve fluency and speed. "Word blindness" was the layman's term in the 70s and 80s for dyslexia and those struggling with literacy. It is a perfect description as this is exactly right – "not seeing words".

The simplest way to test this out is to ask a friend who is a good speller to spell "conscientious", for example. They will start to spell it and as it gets more complicated, their eyes will look up to focus on the word, becoming consciously aware of something that is normally a completely subconscious habit.

The Crucial Step: **The skill you need to develop is the ability to recall a word you have seen before. You simply need to learn how to "see" the word, be able to hold the letters still and then spell it or write it down. The dictionary of these words is built through practice and reading.**

> I recall a five year old that one of the Learning Assistants noticed was exceptional at spelling. She asked the little girl how she did it. "Well, I just imagine I am reading the word on a page, block out all the rest of the page and write down the word." This was so easy and natural for her.

Many who struggle with literacy have a highly developed visual brain with the capability of moving pictures at fantastic speeds, often in 3D (see examples in Chapter 2). Unfortunately, such people are often using the same strategy for words and it doesn't work – words are 2D. When these people recall a word all the letters spin around, change places etc., all out of their conscious awareness. Those who are good at computer games can move images at incredible speeds. This ability to move images quickly may even originate from playing with a toy shape sorter and developing a strategy of "when confused turn it round". This is why young people can often spell long words better than short ones; they have more "stability" on the page. Eventually, this tendency can become generalised into a mental pattern of confusion. As this develops, a young person may not realise what is happening and, after a while, the individual often gives up as they are exhausted. As these young people grow up, this confusion so often manifests as poor behaviour and disaffection, leading to school refusers.

Word recognition is essential for:

- **English:** We have many spelling rules, silent letters, words that break rules and homophones, where the sound of two words is just the same and the spelling is quite different, e.g. eight and ate. This often leads to young people being able to read better than spell.
- **Foreign languages:** Visualising words in different colours for different languages is very helpful. Without visualising words people will have better literacy on one language than another! For example, languages like Spanish are perfectly phonetic and hence an auditory strategy works well, because you write down what you hear. English isn't.
- **Speed reading:** You will never master speed reading at any level without word recognition. Without this, you will inevitably put a greater than necessary stress on the wrong part of your brain. Using phonics alone for reading, you will find that you are sub-vocalising every word and that will inhibit fast reading. As you get more fluent, you will be able to stop fixating on every word and just create pictures of the material you read. The faster you get the more you will retain. Although this might sound counterintuitive, it is a proven fact[45].
- **Coping with different "English" accents**, such as Scottish, West Country, Canadian, American, Australian, Irish, etc. These can make the phonemes sound very different.

- **Those with poor hearing:** Poor physical hearing, deafness (possibly a cochlear implant), low auditory due to infections or glue ear may distort sounds and make phonics difficult.

Even if you have poor physical sight, the mind's eye can be very good for visual recall.

Those people who do well with phonics have also picked up the skill to visualise naturally. In fact that "light bulb" moment, when a child suddenly improves literacy at a young age, may be the moment they have picked up visualising words[46].

> " Henry is eleven and struggles with all aspects of literacy - spelling reading, writing. After twenty minutes he managed to spell seven letter words that were previously unknown to him. He could visualise them and even spell them backwards! My husband and I felt very emotional during the session, as Henry's self-confidence blossomed. We have continued to use this technique at home for five minutes daily and now (two weeks later) he can spell all the days of the week and different words for Mathematics. I am very impressed with this technique and have recommended it to several of the children I teach. This programme should certainly be rolled out in schools." Sarah, B.Ed (Primary School Teacher)

If an individual doesn't experience the "light bulb" moment before the age of seven, things tend to go wrong. Confusion, increased frustration and stress are experienced, which inevitably leads to the child becoming un-grounded. This in turn increases concern in the family and can result in deteriorating behaviour, which often accelerates quite quickly, because the young person realises they can't do what is being asked of them at school. Often, such children then go into the "Identity Jump" (outlined in chapter 5), deciding that "they are stupid," that "people hate them", or adopting many other damaging beliefs.

When an individual becomes un-grounded, the letters will start to move on the page, a downside of their exceptional visual skills. The more they try and the more stressed they get, the faster the letters move and the more Dyslexic they become. Some people call this the Irlen Syndrome, for which coloured glasses or overlays are prescribed. Coloured glasses and overlays may help the external eye, which is essential for reading. However, as glasses work on the cones at the back of the retina[47], they won't help the stability of the mind's eye. On the other hand, grounding will enable you to relax and eliminate visual stress in both the mind's eye *and* the external eye, restoring stability to both and avoiding any stigma in the classroom of having to wear unusual glasses.

Back to brain science for a moment. The occipito-temporal region is where we hold pictures. It is also where we hold images of words. As Sally Shaywitz's research using MRI brain scans, has shown:

"Beginning readers must first analyse a word; skilled readers identify a word instantaneously. The parieto-temporal system works for the novice reader. Slow and analytic, its function seems to be in the early stages of learning to read, that is, in initially analysing a word, pulling it apart and aligning its letters to their sounds. In contrast the occipito-temporal region is the express pathway to reading and is the one used by skilled readers. The more skilled the reader the more they activate this region. It responds very rapidly in less than 150 milliseconds (less than a heartbeat) – to seeing a word; instead of analysing a word, the occipito-temporal area reacts almost instantly to the whole word as a pattern. One brief glance and the word is automatically identified on sight. Not surprisingly, the occipito-temporal region is referred to as the word form area or system.

Here's how we think the word form area works: After a child has analysed and correctly read a word several times, he forms an exact neural model of that specific word; the model (word form) reflecting the word's spelling, its pronunciation and its meaning is now permanently stored in the occipito-temporal system. Subsequently, just seeing the word in print immediately activates the word form and all the relevant information about that word.[48]"

Having gained this new skill of visualising words, as the young person becomes more confident, they will get an added bonus of the feeling of success, which, because it is a feeling is a kinaesthetic experience.

"From an early age I realised that Alistair didn't find reading easy. Alistair suffered from a very nasty dose of chicken pox at eighteen months which the doctors believe got into his ears and affected his hearing for a while.

From the time that he started speaking clearly many people commented on how vivid his imagination was. He would describe how he was going to build aeroplanes and machines with concepts way beyond his years. Yet his reading wasn't progressing and when assessed by the Special Needs teacher, he had dyslexic tendencies. In the visual side of the tests he achieved one of the highest scores she had ever recorded. I spent many hours with Alistair encouraging him; spelling just seemed to frustrate and upset him and he would look at me with a completely lost expression and say 'I can't do it Mummy'. Alistair was always eager to learn and will try his best in everything he does and was finding things so hard.

I found your first book when he was seven. I thought it was written for him. We worked thorough his visual memory pictures and then started to use it for words. The instant difference was amazing. Words which previously caused Alistair many problems he could spell forwards (and backwards) and remember them. He was on the lowest level for class spellings and in one week he went from 7/12 to 16/16, correctly spelling words that he wasn't even supposed to learn as they were deemed too difficult for him. This transformation has been an amazing and incredible journey for Alistair. He has started actually reading books instead of just guessing at the words. A fantastic new world opened up for Alistair; he just started reading road signs, shops signs, the programmes on the telly – he just didn't stop reading things and spelling words. I was so pleased that his confidence is increasing and he told me this week that I can put my hand up now in class and spell the words that the teacher is asking. The first time he achieved top marks in his spelling he was ecstatic.

........eighteen months later: Alistair received the "Special Head Teachers Award" this week for being the only child in his year for getting all his eighteen spellings right for the last three tests. He is such a completely changed boy from the little lad who used to just grab my arm and say "I can't do it Mummy". He now visualises his words quickly by himself each time he sees a new word. He loves spelling and reading now and his literacy skills have increased greatly.

........three years later Alistair, at ten years old, is a friendly, happy little lad. At parents evenings every teacher confirms he is one of the hardest working children in the class. He is still very visual and has imaginative skills which I am sure will always be part of his personality". **Alistair's mother**

Simple Skills #8: Spelling

Spelling using your visual memory is a very simple skill. This section is just a summary. For anyone wanting to improve their spelling, the workbook[49] that goes with this book is recommended. It takes you through a step by step approach to success, attainable by anyone and a great confidence builder. It is available to download free of charge (see page cxxxi for details).

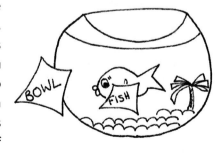

For very young children, the simplest way to encourage this skill is to get very young children to associate words with objects. I do this with a simple post-it pad and felt pen; no expensive resources are needed. Simply label all the objects in the home or the classroom; write "wall" on a post-it on the wall, "window" on window, etc. Refer to them occasionally if you want and don't make a big issue of it – a child will naturally start associating pictures in their head of a window with the word window, for example. If they are playing with bricks you can even stick a label on the bricks.

When young people are first being introduced to words in school or at home, it is invaluable for them to use all their senses - visual, auditory and kinaesthetic, even taste and smell if they are appropriate. A good example of this would be being able to imagine a rose and at the same time smell the flower and see how the word is written. In my experience, it is much more successful to teach fewer words, making use of all the senses rather than to introduce more words in just an auditory mode. It is also essential that we first teach nouns or colours as they activate the occipito-temporal region of the brain. However, almost all high frequency words[50] (45 out of 50) taught to four year olds in the UK and around the English speaking world are not nouns or colours and have no pictures. They are words such as is, on, a, it, no, they, up and went, that will not activate the occipito-temporal region of the brain, where pictures are stored and where fluent readers read from. This instantly puts a young person at a disadvantage if he or she has not already picked up the "natural skill" to visualise words.

Flash cards with a picture of the object and the word written across the object are ideal. If the word is written underneath, above or to the side then the young person has to remember two images and connect them together. Confusion with writing over pictures has never seemed to be a problem. You can very quickly progress to asking the young person to, say, imagine a dragon, show them a post-it with dragon written on it and then ask them to put the letters on the side of the dragon. You need to build up through three, four, five, etc. letters to ensure they remain confident. Everyone can do this.

As imagination is a child's specialist subject and a source of enjoyment, this is easy for them, possibly easier for them than for teachers and parents. This approach does, of course, mean that high frequency words will need to be delayed until the young person is securely visualising nouns and colours. However, it will save an enormous amount of repetitive teaching later. Once young people are confident, ask them to visualise the word on an imaginary whiteboard. You will now find that they can deal with words that have no pictures, including all those high frequency words. Initially we ask the young people to spell the word both forwards and in reverse order – the only way to know for certain that they are actually seeing the letters.

With older young people who are already struggling with SpLDs, you need a little time to take them step by step through the process, while at the same time working with them on remaining grounded and releasing unpleasant emotions. You will also need to engage other family members. As shown in chapter 11, if other family members have similar challenges, this can lead to erroneous beliefs, such as "if dad can't spell either, it must be OK".

Parents, teachers and learning assistants can all teach this skill which, with practice, should only take about an hour. You are developing a new habit here and it is generally accepted that new habits need twenty-eight days practice (although with children I have seen this happen in a far shorter time).

Teaching visually to people with great visual skills, you simply:

- Use exactly the same process for foreign languages, visualising in different colours for different languages, even Chinese characters as they are particularly visual. For French, where there are multiple genders, you can have an added bonus, to visualise female words in pink and male in blue, for example.
- Add a picture to a homophone on a post-it to distinguish between them. For example, add lips to 'ate' and number 8 to 'eight'.
- Visualise the correct spelling with a tick. If a specific word is consistently spelt wrongly, visualise the word with an incorrect spelling, with a big red cross through the middle.
- Add any more visual cues needed for specific topics.

If you have a list of spellings to teach, *never* teach/learn from a list. Copy them out onto individual post-its and address them one at a time. Learning from a list can mean success in a spelling test and an inability thereafter to spell the individual words in context. This is because they are coded in the brain as a list, which means when a single word is needed, they have difficulty locating it.

Again, I really recommend that you download a copy of the workbook[51] that your child can use, so that with some of your help, they will create new habits very quickly.

Simple skills #9: Handwriting

On the subject of writing, we have collected some diverse examples of things people do and simple ways to improve your handwriting:

- Some people prefer to write in capital letters – in business this is taken as shouting. Some put capital letters in the middle of a word.
- Some leave out the spaces between words.
- People with poor handwriting may believe there is something wrong with their hand, arm, elbow, brain etc. and there is nothing that can be done.
- Some write badly, consciously or unconsciously, to cover up bad spelling.
- People with poor literacy will copy, one letter at a time from the board in school. This is slow, they lose their place, make mistakes and get a stiff neck too.
- In English, we have three sets of lettering; capitals, lower case and joined up. Different schools have different strategies about which to teach at what age.

Young children, who don't develop the ability to visualise letters won't know which way round they should be and may start to develop Dyslexic tendencies before the age of seven. They can only do this because they haven't learnt to visualise them the right way round and keep them still. The lower case letters, p, q, b and d are all mirror images of exactly the same letter. Lucky children grow out of it while others never do. This really can't be left to chance.

There are some interesting facts about capital letters worth considering, particularly so that you may understand more fully why some children in fact prefer capitals. When young people read cartoon books, it is often not just for the pictures, but because the speech bubbles are often in capital letters. Most keyboards are uppercase and many young people manage computers well. Capital letters are more distinct than lower case and, if you suffer from letters moving or shaking on the page, no capital letters can turn around and make another letter. Additionally, nearly half of them can flip around horizontally without causing problems e.g. A, H, I, X. Others turn around in the vertical plane, for example B and C. So even if the young person in question is in the habit of turning letters around, they would not notice the difference with these. Some people prefer joined up writing because that gives the word more stability and joined up letters don't turn around. However, books aren't normally written in joined up writing. There are hundreds of fonts and some have the letters formed completely differently, e.g. a and ɑ. My strategy is to let people start, at least initially, with whatever form of writing they prefer, in order to help them gain confidence.

To begin improving a child's handwriting, first look at the physiology of the person. If they are looking down, maybe collapsed on the desk, they will be in their emotions and internal dialogue, probably telling themselves "your handwriting is terrible". Confirming how bad they are at writing will create poor handwriting; we do like to be right! Next help them learn this "magical" skill:

✓ Hold up a card with good clear writing on it and ask the young person to copy down the words, <u>without</u> looking at the paper on which they're writing.

✓ You want it written exactly the same as on the card, not converted into their own handwriting. Once their brain gets what you are requesting, they will probably produce better handwriting than normal, even without looking at the paper.

✓ This is an ideal skill to assist with copying down from the board and improving hand writing. It is fast, causes less stress and, with a little practise, should produce neat results. I personally used this strategy all through school and University. The non-writing hand can be used as a marker, moving down the page as the individual writes to keep lines even. By copying what is seen, writing will dramatically improve.

✓ The next step is to visualise a word and write it, again without looking at the paper. Prior to this, the individual needs to get grounded and be sitting well, so the words are seen clearly – slouching means images can't be seen easily. With practise and Increasing confidence, the individual should be able to lookup and down as they wish, knowing where to find those words which are causing uncertainty.

✓ You can, of course, add in some BrainGym[52] exercises such as lazy 8 or alphabet 8 to improve fluency of writing and brain integration.

✓ Remember: Look up. See the word. Write it down.

If you struggle to get words on paper, but really know what you want to say, check what is actually happening. Some people construct a sentence in their head, then realise that they can't spell a few words, so make another sentence and discover another couple of words they can't spell. Doing this rapidly creates a "brain freeze" where you are unable to put any words on paper. We had a post-graduate student explain that this is what used to happen before she learnt to spell visually. Now she is a successful lecturer and her literacy difficulties belong to the past. As your spelling and writing improves brain freezes will disappear too.

I always remember the first autistic child I helped with literacy. He was in a class full of eleven year olds, in his own world, tearing up bits of plastic with his hands and carefully protecting the bits. He was calm in his obsession. I watched and, after a while, asked him if it was a dinosaur he had there and, why he had his hands around it. He pointed to the nearby open window and an incoming breeze.

I demonstrated with my hands how to stand it up on the windowsill and then on the grass bank outside. I asked him about the size and colour of the dinosaur, keeping him focused on his picture. I then showed him a post-it with 'T-rex' written on it, which I held in his eye-line. I asked him to slip the word onto his picture and spell T-Rex. Bless him, he spelt, to my amazement, 'Tyrannosaurus', I could hardly believe what I heard. He then spelt it in reverse order! Before I started, I had no idea that dinosaurs were his specialist subject or that, at the age of eleven, he had not spelt any word in his class for the last six months. I had just given him an important **how to** and from then on, he saw all his words on the side of a dinosaur, staying relaxed and with little effort.

Simple Skills #10: Reading

Reading automatically improves once you have word recognition. To assist with this process, notice where you are holding the book. Try this little exercise:

Put the book in your lap and read it, out loud or to yourself, as you prefer. Notice what it feels like in your tummy as you read the book. Now get yourself grounded, prop the book up a little and repeat the exercise. Hold the book right up in front of you and repeat it again. Notice the difference. In the story in Chapter 17, George said he felt sad looking down and trying to read. However, it was "possible" when he looked up. In Chapter 11, Jim couldn't even see the letters when he looked down at a book, as it triggered off so much negativity. You may even find it useful to get a small bookstand to help you if you have a lot to read[53]. Try to find the best position for you!

If you have any symptoms of the letters moving, get yourself grounded and relaxed again. In addition, try different positions for the book and don't attempt to read until you have the letters still, as this is exhausting and really not good for your health.

I have noticed many young people get so stressed attempting to read that they stop breathing. Remind them that punctuation is a space for breathing, as it dramatically improves reading and the child's ability to maintain a sense of what they have read.

> Amon was ten years old and was really struggling with reading. He would start a sentence then stumble over a word. Then as you saw his face start to look stressed, he would stumble on more words, not stop at punctuation, have no idea what he read and be gasping for breath. I found the answer for him by explaining that he was expected to breathe when meeting full stops, commas etc., when reading. I added that he needed to stop and "let go" of all that tension into his roots, when he first started to stumble. Within ten minutes he was reading fluently and with expression. What a change!

As your reading improves, you will be putting more words into the occipito-temporal region of your brain. Going forward, you will be able to access them far more easily for spelling. The more you can relax, the more fluent you will become and as your confidence builds you will be able to lower the book. If coloured overlays or coloured glasses help, use them to start with and then see if you can achieve the same with just imagining that the paper is coloured. Do whatever works best for you until you can read to yourself fluently.

While you are developing this skill, you may find that some emotions come up which are connected with struggles from your past. Don't panic, simply let them go into your roots, get yourself another lake and a magnet or a waste bin, and watch all the emotions disappear. Then fill yourself up with your new found confidence. Now that you have a new skill, a new way of reading, these emotions belong to your past and can be released.

As reading improves, you may find that it is better than your spelling. Use the following skill to help even things out: When you find a word which you don't know how to spell, ask yourself the question "If I was reading that word, what would it look like?" You will probably be able to visualise it.

Speed reading is a further layer to be learned. To do this successfully, you need to stop sub-vocalisation (your inner voice). You also need to stop obsessing over words and going back over and over what you have read. You need to scan lines and even pages of text to extract

the meaning and create pictures for your memory. You can find more information about this through speed reading specialists.

Just a word about reading aloud. It is no different to reading to yourself. The audience and the emotions it brings up in you are the problem. Start with a very passive audience that will not criticise you – a small baby or the dog are ideal candidates. Stay grounded and just read as if you were reading to yourself. As you get more relaxed and calmer about reading, you will find you are naturally saying one word or phrase while your mind is reading a few words ahead. As your confidence builds, progress to reading aloud to people who support you. Soon enough, you will be confident enough to read to anyone.

If you have seen the film, "The King's Speech"[54], you'll recall the speech problem was portrayed in the film as being about childhood memories, of being teased and ridiculed. Watching real life footage of the King, it can be seen he was visibly stressed and un-grounded. When we are un-grounded many things don't work well.

Proof readers have the skill to look at text and the spelling errors just "jumps out at them". This is just another skill to learn with practice.

Make this into a story – How can someone go from being a poor reader to a fluent one just by reading Harry Potter?

Chapter 14: Higher Levels of Grounding

Now you have some experience of grounding, this chapter will help you develop this skill further. This skill is especially valuable for several forms of SpLD. There are various levels of grounding that you can achieve and all of these will build on and reinforce one another. The model of levels I use is the Neuro-logical levels[55] that can be applied to almost any circumstance in life, helping you to put a structure around your experience. You can think of any experience in life of terms of:

* the environment - **where** am I, **when** did I do this?
* behaviour - **what** did I do?
* capability - **how** do I do this?
* beliefs and values - **why** am I doing this?
* Identity - **who** am I? How do I see myself?

The Neuro-logical Levels of Grounding

Physical grounding you can test out for yourself any time by walking barefoot on grass or in the sea – this is the environmental level. Both of these are very grounding. An easy time to notice whether you are **physically** grounded or not, is while playing sports. Sportsmen and women are often very grounded, although they may use different words to express this state. For example grounding will help you:

* Befriend horses – they won't like an un-grounded rider.
* Be strong to resist a rugby tackle.
* Shoot penalties (football and American football).
* Converting tries (rugby).

- Preparing to hit a ball (in cricket, baseball or golf).
- Target shooting.
- All forms of gymnastics (whether or not they are physically in contact with the ground), wrestling and yoga.

After physical grounding you can consider un-grounded **behaviours**. When you see someone as not very grounded, you are probably referring to their **behaviour**; what is happening to them? They may do inappropriate things and even behave in a way that really isn't like them. They may be very wobbly, clumsy and even un-grounded in particular parts of the body, or their speech. For example, the feeling of being un-grounded from your knees down has given rise to the popular expression "my knees are turning to jelly".

Grounding is a simple skill to learn, through increased awareness, giving you an invaluable **capability** to improve many aspects of your life. As you practise more, you will learn more about grounding. Grounding is a skill, a **how to**. Like anything else, however, some people find the skill easier than others. That said, everyone can learn it and make great increases in their capability. Realising what un-grounds you and **how to** get grounded will also increase your skills.

Individual **beliefs and values,** however, may undermine developing this skill. For example, if you believe that you "will never be successful" or that "you shouldn't be on the planet", it will be much harder to stay grounded. Beliefs and values provide reinforcement that support or inhibit particular **capabilities**. Once you believe you can do something it will be a lot easier.

Un-grounded beliefs can be held so strongly that they lead to an un-grounded **identity**; "I don't feel like me anymore" or "I hate myself".

Those who have had a close call with death or a traumatic birth may also report they "don't feel they are all here". How individuals perceive themselves to be is what gives them a sense of their role in society.

Those with SpLDs are often very un-grounded and the more stress they have about their situation, the more un-grounded they become. However, it is a simple technique to teach people how to feel more connected with the earth that holds so much for them.

Simple skill #11: Being Present in Your Body

To be fully engaged with your body, you need to be in the present moment. One thing that often un-grounds us is being in the past, with concerns and worries about things that have happened or alternatively being in the future, planning, worrying, running "what if" scenarios. These racing thoughts tend to go faster and faster, like a mouse on a wheel. This is often a particular problem in the middle of the night when you are trying to sleep.

Focusing on our breathing enables us to bring our thoughts into the present, and not focus on what happened five minutes, five days or even five years ago. This is such an essential skill, yet one that we may often neglect. Notice how you breathe, without moving your shoulders, into the bottom of your lungs exercising your diaphragm. As you inhale, your belly expands, as you exhale, it contracts[56].

Listen to your breathing, listen to silence, focus on and heighten your senses. Then select a positive emotion to enjoy, perhaps gratitude, love, or calm. These are all you need to keep you in the present and grounded.

Next, shift your focus down into your lower hara, your centre, around your belly button, and see how that busyness goes away. Moving any busyness down out of our body and into the ground will give even more relief. This will help you to be in your body, noticing what is happening in the present. As human beings we operate best when connected to the earth.

"Mindfulness" approaches, which are derived from Buddhist philosophy, are being increasingly used in a wide range of Western medical settings. This is increasingly true as the research base outlining the benefits of this approach grows further. There are clear parallels with the concepts of grounding and greater awareness, through the focus on what is happening in the present moment. You are not judging, reflecting or thinking. You are simply observing the moment in which you find yourself. Moments are like breaths. Each breath is replaced by the next breath. To give you a little sample[57]:

- ✓ **Start by being aware of your breath, you know it comes and goes. It is like the end of one wave from among the endless ocean waves. They continue to come and disappear to be followed by another, another and another. They come. They disappear. They come, they end, they flow back to be covered by another incoming wave. You can hear the sound. Its rhythm puts the mind into a trance, and you go far away and wherever you go, there you are.**
- ✓ **The ebb and flow and the constant sound of the waves can carry you away as you sit here.**
- ✓ **Like your thoughts, each breath comes and goes. Even as you are aware of your breathing, your mindfulness of your breath comes and goes. You've changed nothing and with each breath there's a new present moment.**

✓ **The previous breath is no longer. The next breath does not yet exist. There is only the present breath you are taking.** If you worry about your next breath, or dwell too long on the past breath, you've lost the moment with the present breath you are taking.

✓ **The past is gone. You can do nothing about it. The future is not yet here so there is no need to worry about it. The only gift of life you have is now. That's why they call this gift of life, our present.**

Now notice your personal space, that invisible space around you that is part of you, thinking perhaps of the energy field of a magnet as an example. Those who travel in crowded public transport will be all too familiar with the feeling of others being in their personal space. Some sensitive young people are very aware of needing their personal space and this tip will help them in crowded situation.

✓ **Notice that space and claim it as yours. If others are physically too close, imagine you can change the vibration level of your space, so it can co-exist and not interact with other energy fields. Notice how this feels more comfortable as you claim the space you have a perfect right to.**

Simple Skill #12: Our True Essence

Don't let SpLDs have any negative effect on who you are; these are just what you do; they are behaviours, not your identity. Now you are more grounded, more present and validated, you will have a growing sense of your real essence and how you manifest that. To clarify this in every cell in your body try this short visualisation:

✓ Imagine a single drop of liquid that represents how your true essence looks, sound and feels.
✓ Wait until your inner wisdom has had time to present to your conscious mind a suitable image. I like to think of mine as a pearl shaped drop of liquid, held together by a thin translucent membrane of swirling colours. Whatever you imagine that is right for you.
✓ Now gently take this drop of your true essence and drop it on the top of your head, feeling it ripple though every cell in your body, resetting every cell to be fully in touch with your true essence.
✓ Notice how this feels.

For Young Children

Here are two favourites for young children:

Cup your hands together in front of your belly and just twist from side to side gently and then bounce slightly if you like. You will feel energy clearing in your body. You can also let your hands just swing and imagine you are a corkscrew winding down and down into the ground. You will feel your feet getting heavier and more connected to the ground.

You can also check which way your core (that little imaginary ball in the centre of you) is spinning. Ask a child to show you with their hand which way it is going. Spinning forwards creates an ungrounded state, but spinning backwards is very grounding. Wobbling is just that, it makes you feel very wobbly like a spinning top when it slows down. Adjust this natural spin, using your hand as a guide to your subconscious, until you are comfortable.[58]

Chapter 15: Memory Skills

I am always surprised by the reports I hear of young people who have poor short term memory. I wonder whether they have ever had any training in how to remember things, and whether indeed they are motivated to remember what is being asked of them. Maybe they can remember every kick of the last football match, but nothing about the last geography lesson – surely this is telling us something quite different. This chapter gives you some memory tools to work with, but at heart this is not always a memory issue; rather, it is one of motivation and engagement.

Simple Skills #13: Comprehension

This is a very visual skill that is almost never taught. To do comprehension and be able to summarise easily, you simply create pictures of what you are reading.

✓ To start with, find an audio recording of a very graphic story, like Alice in Wonderland. Listen to the story and make up pictures to remember what you have heard. If you are reading to a young child, you can take any story and add a few prompts to help trigger their memory – this is like stage management for the brain. In this example the brackets [] indicate the stage management instructions: There were lots of tin solders marching along the road [suggest that the child should attempt to notice how many, how many per row, how many rows]. They were wearing blue and silver uniforms, with a black stripe up the trousers, [put that in your picture]. As they came past you noticed a teddy bear marching with them. He was wearing a blue uniform and a silver cap [add the bear to your picture].

✓ Now you have a picture of everything you have heard you will be able to answer questions about the pictures you have created in your mind's eye.

✓ As your reading improves you will be able to read and create pictures at the same time, without any prompts. Comprehension will automatically become easier.

Simple Skills #14: Telling the Time

Reading the time from a standard clock with hands is complicated, because there seems to be no structure for what the hands mean. By contrast, digital clocks are so much easier to understand. Traditional clocks will be around for a long while, however, so here is a useful tip.

Using a clock on which you can move the hands, select say 2:30. Now ask the person you are helping to visualise 2:30. Get them to recall it on a piece of paper or move the hands on a clock. Do the same for several different times, say 8:15, 12:00 etc. Each time ask them to visualise the clock face and recall it. As they get more confident try asking them a few times that they haven't visualised. This step by step strategy normally produces a breakthrough; again you are employing their visual memory. The Helen Arkell Teaching clock[59] has great visual cues, with different colours and sections.

Simple Skills #15: Sequencing and Short Term Memory

Young people are often labelled as having poor short term memory. They may get given this label because they can't remember a story (for example, see skill #13), or perhaps because they can't remember a number of tasks they have been asked to do.

The first thing to do is check the language you are using. Visual people will be able to construct a series of visual images to help them memorise things. If you use words like "before", "and don't forget", then the images will be out of order and they will indeed forget things. For example, if you say, "Put your coat on, get the bus and don't forget your PE kit", they will have their coat on and be on the bus before they think of the PE kit. A simple change of language can put things in order of action. For instance, a set of instructions to collect your PE kit, put your coat on and only then to get the bus may prove far more successful. This is particularly true in the case of a very literal individual, which is often seen, for example, with Asperger's syndrome.

However, not everyone may create visuals when you ask them to do a list of things. So when you have time, get them to imagine a series of pictures, running from left to right for example:

✓ **See the alarm clock going off in the morning**
✓ **Next see yourself jumping out of bed**
✓ **Then see yourself coming downstairs and eating your breakfast**
✓ **Then see yourself going upstairs having a wash and brushing your hair**

✓ **Now see yourself getting dressed, now see yourself putting your outdoor coat and shoes on and leaving the house.**

Use straightforward language and ask them to see all those pictures like a video, running through it a few times. You will find this really helps a visual child get things in the right order.

> One autistic child was in the room and not engaged in conversation when I was explaining this strategy to his mother. He had never mastered language and had no sign of recognition about what we were saying. The next morning he put his outdoor shoes on before trying to get out the house for school – it was the first time he had done this, in the right order.

Sequencing is essentially the skill to remember a list and act upon it. You may ask a young person to do a number of things and they only end up doing the last one.

You will know that many of the people who specialise in memory skills use a series of anchors and pictures to remember thousands of things, so we teach the simplest versions[60].

Another thing to consider is whether you have poor short term memory for everything or just things that don't interest you. For example can you remember what happened in a recent television programme you watched? If you can, then your challenge is not short term memory. Rather, it is more about what catches your interest and to what you can pay attention most easily. You may also consider the state you were in when you were experiencing something you wanted to remember. Everyone has experienced leaving the room to collect something and forgetting what it was you went for. Take yourself back to the original environment and there is the answer immediately. There is much published about state-dependent learning, which includes factors such as environment, emotional state, etc.

Simple Skill #16: Numbers

Many people struggle with numeracy, and some statistics show this is even worse than literacy. In my part of the UK, the issues of poor numeracy and literacy are the two main reasons for not employing people being interviewed for their first job.

> "The visualisation which you taught me worked a dream, and also not letting the numbers fluster me seems to make a big difference. I can remember telephone numbers and page numbers much more easily (and write them down in the correct order!) if I glue the numbers down! It feels a bit odd to do it, yet it works! The numbers used to randomly appear (and disappear!!) as very pale white spectres, and now they're flushed pink, larger, clear 3D characters! Thank you so much for this insight into how to keep numbers still. They have been running rings around me all my life (and worse, I was regularly severely told off by my very loving, well-meaning and extremely frustrated ex-forces mathematician father. Scaaaaarey!) I am now proud to be able to tell you that it's the 17th day of the 10th month, not the 10th of the 17th. And I'm on page 142, not 241 or 412 or 214, of my Brookmyre book. :D

As a Maths graduate, I know it is impossible to do almost any level of maths without being able to visualise numbers. So I teach people to visualise numbers and keep them still in just the same way as letters. If they move, don't forget to get grounded and release any stress into the ground. Look at a number and see if you can visualise it, perhaps adding it to a word. So if you can visualise the word cat you can visualise six cats. This simple step is great progress for some. Again you need to keep them still.

Many young people complain that they don't understand the strange squiggles we use for numbers, so this explanation helps them. Numbers were created by the Phoenician merchants as a technique used for counting. You will see from the following diagram that the number 1 has one angle, number 2 has two, number 3 has three etc. The number 0 was not part of the original set and added later; of course it has no angles.

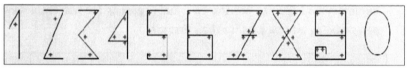

In later times these numbers became the numbers we are all familiar with today.

1 2 3 4 5 6 7 8 9 0

Just showing this to someone who is struggling with numbers will be helpful, they can just add up the stars if they wish. They can start to do mental arithmetic in their head using the Phoenician numbers and quite literally start counting stars on them for addition.

Other techniques like number bonds, counting lines, counting beads or an abacus can also be visualised.

A parent walked up to me after a training session in the Netherlands and asked whether I could shine any light on how his son could be great at maths and confused at the same time. His son knew what 10 - 7 was immediately, and asked what 10 apples minus 7 apples would be, had no idea. When asked how this very visual child was attempting to do the calculation, the boy said, "the answer came in a flash when it was just numbers, and when apples were added, I see lots of them and just got confused. Once he realised why he was having so much trouble he was able to organise the 10 apples into a single basket and the calculation was easy.

Children with great visual skills may get confused when a maths problem includes objects. The lower levels of the maths exams have a lot more words and the words can trigger too much information. Remember this child has great visual skills and when you say ten apples he will be visualising those, and he may have more than one TV screen and have 10 apples on each, so when he tries to take away 7 apples, confusion breaks out. Help him to get grounded and ask him to tell you exactly what he is seeing in his mind's eye. His answer will probably be unique and with that information, you will be able to help him.

For multiplication and division, number triangles are very useful. They are often taught in secondary school and pupils are not encouraged to visualise them. This one means:

2 times 5 = 10 and
10 divided by 2 = 5 and
10 divided by 5 = 2

Of course 2 times 5 = 10 and 5 times 2 = 10. So you only need to learn half of the ones you usually do.

Simple Skills #17: Study Skills

By this stage, you will be realising how you can help your visually talented young people, utilising those things at which they excel. Here are a few more examples and you will find many more available to you:

- Mind Maps[61].
- Geography – Learn the names of countries, capital cities, mountain ranges etc. with the aid of simple maps.
- Biology – learn the names of bones etc. by writing the name on a diagram of the human body. Don't use speech bubble labelling which is confusing.
- Formulas are easy to learn visually, provided of course, they are kept static.
- Visual Reasoning - Recently we did a research project at the University of Bedfordshire with Computer Science undergraduates, under the control of their Lecturer, Herbert Daly. We taught the students visual reasoning for their main course work, HTML programming and UML. The students measurably benefited in their tests[62].
- Speed reading.

"Thank you for helping to build our daughter's confidence in English. She achieved two A*s for English Language and English Literature in her GCSEs and, as a result, now has the confidence to tackle Government Studies and Politics at A level which is very essay-based – you made a huge difference and we are very appreciative". J Bond

Chapter 16: Moving Blocks to Success

This chapter looks at the causes of blocks and confusion, in particular, SpLD, life events other peoples' energy and information overload. It encourages you to simply clear out what you no longer need. All the topics mentioned in this chapter are likely to lower a person's self esteem, making them feel stupid. Over time, this will lead to blockages in their energy channels.

How Do We Get So Blocked?

Blocks hold you back. A young person who struggles with SpLD will probably have decided he or she is stupid and every word they read or write incorrectly will ultimately reinforce the internal message, "Stupid, told you so!" It will seem impossible to improve and the very thought of trying will often upset the child and block their energy.

In addition to this, your energy channels can get blocked by accidents, operations, traumas, negative reactions (either yours or those of others), allergic reactions, or by picking up other peoples' energy.

However, once they realise you can learn a new skill; simply **how to** release blocks, more things may fall into place than you expect.

When working with a young person diagnosed with Dyslexia and Dyspraxia, I had taught him to spell visually. I then questioned him about his Dyspraxia and how that manifested. He seemed to be generally wobbly, so I taught him the Lake and the Magnet guided story. He suddenly had a sharp pain in his arm that lasted just a few seconds and then it was fine. Afterwards he told me he'd just had a plaster cast removed from a broken arm. He had in fact managed to clear his blocked energy in just a few seconds which would aid his healing.

I recall a client recently who came to a workshop only because he wanted to help his son and said "You do realise I am going to have to face my greatest fear: to have to spell a word in public". Not surprising as of course this had immediately triggered his "I feel stupid" programming. Feeling you're stupid will block anyone's progress. Once he became aware of this simple skill and all that he needed to do was practise, his blocks disappeared.

Blocks will always be energetic and may manifest physically, mentally, consciously. They are all messages from your subconscious which is finding ways to keep you informed as to what is really happening.

Anyone who has experienced body work will know that unblocking energy can be painful for a moment, followed by a feeling of relief. When we have been in plaster or in traction, unable to move for a period of time with a broken bone, our energy becomes stagnant and blocked. Physiotherapy is thankfully the normal course of treatment. I hope you are realising, you can also make a major contribution to your own healing through your thoughts and your understanding of energy.

Simple Skill #18: Reversing the Identity Jump

The identity jump (explained in chapter 5) is just one of the ways young people often get blocked. Most with SpLDs have years of programming from themselves and others about how they are failing. Their identity becomes locked into failure and their self-esteem drops. The great thing about the identity jump is that once you understand it, you can reprogram it into being a positive jump. However, we can start to change all this into a positive spiral with a few simple techniques.

Notice what people are good at. Earlier you read about some of the quite exceptional skills that people struggling with SpLD have, but may not have even noticed. To combat this, start validating people when and where they excel. Ensure you are giving praise, in a way your words will really resonate with the person, or else it will be dismissed and, worse still, seen as patronising. Don't say things like "you are an exceptional son/daughter" as that is an identity level statement they won't believe. Offer praise at the environmental or behavioural level and be specific and factual. For instance, one might say: "I love that picture; the colours in it are gorgeous especially the way the blue and green work together." This way, the person develops their own identity.

One further idea: take the trouble to praise the everyday things. Many years ago, I came across this tale and I have recalled it often. Mum was returning from a parenting class about positive praise and how to deliver it. Her son, who was drinking from a coke bottle, put it on the table and rested the top on it. The mum said "Thanks for putting the top back, we won't lose it". When her son started to tighten the cap she said "That's great, it will keep its fizz". When he put it in the fridge she said "Excellent, it will keep fresh for tomorrow". At that point, the child was looking both pleased and confused at the same time, announcing he was off to bed. His mother said, "It's so nice when you take yourself to bed without me having to remind you!" As this story shows, if you start building up praise at a behavioural level, the young person's identity and self esteem will naturally develop.

I recall the story about Frank recounted in the Preface to this book. When I first met him his self esteem was really low. Well it would be - he was fifteen years old, had been in special education all his life and still couldn't spell or read a single word. As soon as I started teaching him how to spell visually, through his very capable visual memory, his self esteem started to grow and all his other symptoms, such as poor personal hygiene, disinterest in class, etc. started to drift away – just because he was feeling better about himself.

Simple skill #19: Changing Limiting Beliefs

Finding a new perspective is so powerful and so simple, much like looking into a large marble and turning it around to see different images of the same thing. From one side you may see one thing and from another something quite different. This book you are holding is one of the **New Perspectives** series of books, designed to help people discover just that - a new perspective. Seeing exceptional visual skills running in families is empowering. Seeing the negative symptoms as being genetic is limiting. Take a different perspective on these limiting beliefs and you will see how easily the family can help each other learn new skills.

For example, a child who argues very eloquently about almost everything may be cursed by his parents, yet applauded as having an amazing brain for solving problems in business when he or she is older. Such children possess an ability to see things from different perspectives – an ability of considerable value in life. The common post-it was created when a batch of glue didn't work well and someone looked for a different perspective. They investigated what other uses there could be for glue that didn't quite work.

When you realise you have a belief you don't like, sit back, relax:

- ✓ **Imagine a symbol in front of you that represents that belief.**
- ✓ **Imagine grounding the symbol down into the ground and letting all the energy of that belief just disappear into the ground for recycling.**
- ✓ **If you detect any blocks to letting go of this, just imagine the blocks and toss them into the ground too.**
- ✓ **When you have finished, just fill up the space with gold energy.**
- ✓ **Check you can now look past the challenge and see a new perspective.**

Picking up Other People's Energy

When you pick up energy that is not your own, you can be left feeling quite strange, not like you at all and often exhausted.

Now notice your own experience:

- When someone you are talking to is negative and miserable, what happens to you and to them? The normal answer to this is that you feel exhausted whilst the other person goes away feeling better having dumped their stuff on you!
- When talking to someone happy and energised, how do you feel?

- When someone really upsets you, notice how you feel afterwards.
- Do you ever feel like a sponge for energy that is not your own?
- When you go into a meeting or a particular room/place, can you sense the energy in the room?
- What is it like when you go into a place you don't like, such as a hospital, graveyard or a scene of a traumatic accident?
- What non-verbal clues do you pick up when someone is talking to you?

Many people regularly pick up the energy of others, particularly when the other person is in distress and you are a sensitive person. This is often very obvious to people such as doctors, dentists, counsellors, care workers, nurses and emergency workers. Can you

notice your child picking up other energies (including yours) and becoming most uncomfortable? Counsellors, for example, use a supervision framework that enables them to work through any issues that their clients trigger in them. Many other people including teachers, parents and other children have had no such training and the effect on them can be significant. The great benefit from using the simple skills outlined in this book is that you will learn to release much of this energy instantly without external assistance.

When we are born we are open to energy in our environment.

Children who have been spending long periods of time in hospital at a very young age may have picked up a lot of energy that is not their own. When a child is seriously ill, parents will project energy into their space out of concern, which is understandable. However, that energy may remain with an individual and still be there years later.

You can easily catch other people's emotional states. If a friend or work colleague is frustrated, you can catch that frustration to which you will react, either from your own perspective, or more likely from theirs. Think for a moment about times when you picked up energy and acted from someone else's perspective. This, for instance, is a very common habit within families. I have regularly tested out the notion with my puppy. Like most puppies he steals things, running off wagging his tail furiously, enormously pleased with himself. If I get angry with him, he gets angry with me – frighteningly so. If I keep calm, get grounded, ask him to sit down, he doesn't get angry and with a little help from the reward tin he will give up his treasure. With a little patience, the whole process becomes quicker and everyone is happy. So he has been teaching me how to keep calm, whatever happens. The alarming thing is that the anger he demonstrated was my own! He was picking up my anger and acting as I would. Of course, multiple children in a family will be constantly picking up each other's stuff and acting as if they were one of their siblings.

Intuition Development

We have all had experiences of knowing things and not being able to rationalise why or how we know; you may express this as a gut feeling, or just a hunch. According to Dr. Jonas Edward Salk, "Your intuition shows your logical mind where to look". The strength of our intuition, however, depends on how much we are open to its energy and take notice of it. This can vary from person to person. Some people might, with little trouble, effectively develop their intuition. Alternatively, a person might be closed and in fact suppress such skills. As such, some people will be more aware of their intuition than others.

People know what being "in your head" is like – the sense that everything in your life needs to have a reason, you have to understand it and make an intellectual choice. Sometimes we intuitively know things, if we are listening to ourselves.

My experience of people with SpLD is that they are very often have highly developed intuition. They certainly know things you would not expect and at a very young age. For example, they will pick up discontinuities between what someone says and what they mean. This can be very confusing for a young child.

Do You Recognise This?

People with SpLD are often are just overwhelmed by too much information and can't focus. This causes stress, being un-grounded and further confusion. Recognising stress is very important for helping those with an SpLD.

Just consider this simple little story. "I was dusting the lounge and came across a plant which seemed to be pot-bound, so I went to the garden shed to get another pot. Crossing the lawn I noticed the grass was quite long so I got the mower out of the shed. There wasn't any petrol so I went off to the garage to get more fuel. Standing in the queue to pay, I met a neighbour who asked me round for coffee to tell me about her mother. Whilst drinking the coffee, I wondered 'Will I ever finish dusting the lounge?' Do you have stories of your own like this where events, or thoughts, take you down a completely different path from that which you had planned? Imagine doing this type of chain reaction in your head, at speed all day long.

Look at the cartoon as representing your thought patterns. You start off with one idea and the actions arising from that. Then you move on to another idea with its own few actions and so on.

Just think about looking through a pile of papers for something, with each paper creating another four thoughts before you turn to the next. Add to this the routes that sidetrack you as mentioned above.

Anyone who thinks primarily in pictures will very rapidly become overwhelmed and inundated with thousands of their own thoughts. This results in the person becoming un-grounded and going into a spin. The same feelings might arise if you have too many e-mails arriving every day.

Now, imagine little doors within your head which can open and reveal information you want. I know if I get focused on one topic before taking a break, my subconscious will continue to work on the topic, offering up all sorts of good ideas. This is helpful if one door opens on one topic. But what happens if numerous doors are open simultaneously? Here, we become awash with information that we can't possibly process fully, and we will quickly feel overwhelmed.

Think of a time when you are in a state of flow and working on a particular topic. How long does it take to get back to that state after an interruption? It may be five, ten or even twenty minutes. If you are continually interrupting yourself you will never enter a state of flow and will feel quite bewildered.

Ben had just won the A2 level History Prize, but was really struggling to pass his written exams. Whilst I was talking with him, he managed to realise what was going on. When he looked at the question, he immediately thought of five or six different ways he could approach it. Each of those answer streams set off chains of thought. With the stress of the exam room he was immediately into overload and took fifteen minutes to get his thoughts into order, fifteen minutes he didn't have to spare on each question.

I taught him to ground the paper and ground himself after entering the exam room and when reading the question. Even in his imagination he realised how this simple skill would help him. I also encouraged him by adding that, when he has a job where he needs to see problems from dozens of different angles, he will be invaluable. Just for the moment when he sees lots of possible answers to an exam question, he needs to keep that grounded. Once focused, he can then write and record what is needed for the examiner to assess his capabilities and for him to pass his exam.

Being somewhere on the spectrum of those with SpLD can mean a mind in overdrive, always busy, with all the 'brain doors' open to the world with the volume turned up! Much of the information you are receiving you may not even understand and certainly have no idea how to stop. This hurts and it's therefore not surprising that this leads, in some cases, to head banging. In House Rules, Joseph described his brain as "Being like a camera that could record the whole world at once – every sight, sound, feelings, tastes and smells[63]". This isn't very helpful if trying to focus on a single conversation, however. This level of activity easily blocks your energy flow.

Of course on the other side of the coin are the superpowers we see in our young people. They can:

- Be intuitive, clairvoyant and clairaudient.
- Know exactly what Mum is doing upstairs.
- React when what someone says doesn't match what they are thinking. For example, noticing when Mum is crying and saying everything's fine.
- Pick up conversations you don't expect them to.
- React to people's energy, especially when they are not grounded – "when mum comes towards me it feels like very hot asphalt when she is just a few steps away[64]".
- Be very aware of their personal space.
- Demonstrate enormous information recall, even for stuff they really don't want to see, like monsters.
- Be very intelligent in a way not measurable by current standards and method.

A little boy I met recently realised he had superpowers and calmly said, "You know Superman and Spiderman? Nobody asks them about their superpowers. Did they have to go to school?"

Simple skill #20: Feeling Overwhelmed

When people feel overwhelmed, they may report that there are thousands of things going on in or above their heads. This can start with a mild confusion, but might eventually progress to feeling overwhelmed, bewildered or possibly even blanking out. The opposite of this is feeling relaxed and focused.

Now notice your own experience:

- What happens to trigger you into this confused state? Is it just being too busy and having too many interruptions?
- What is this state like and what emotions come up for you?
- When in this state, what do you sense in your body?
- How do you change to being relaxed?

It is really useful to keep a diary for a few days and note down what triggers the confusion and emotions you experience, and how you "let go" of them.

Taking the examples above; let's use a pile of papers or your e-mails to imagine:

- ✓ **Grounding the pile of papers or e-mails all that energy down into the ground - after all, they are only papers and messages.**
- ✓ **Remaining grounded and letting all these thoughts just pass through you.**
- ✓ **Trusting that your inner wisdom won't let you overlook anything important.**
- ✓ **Focusing on the task in hand and not become overloaded.**

✓ **With metaphors you can start shutting some of those doors, leaving open only the ones you select. You can also release to the lake and a magnet anything you don't currently need.**

Now think about what you notice in your young person. The challenge with all SpLDs is to notice how stuck someone is in a particular behaviour. Help them to compare and contrast how it feels to be unstuck, then help them develop skills so they can have a choice. People have reported that some days it feels like being plugged into the mains with so much going on in their heads and no idea what it is. Again grounding will help this, as they can pass all this excess activity down into the ground and run simple skill #23, with particular emphasis on clearing their telepathic channels, around their eyes.

Simple skills #21: Scared of Faces

One frequently reported symptom is poor eye contact and that often turns out to be a real fear of faces.

There are a number of useful things it is worth considering

- The human face changes extremely rapidly and we have thousands of different expressions. This can cause overload of information. However, a dog or cat has relatively few so this may be an easier starting point. Or, you  could start with "Thomas the Tank Engine[65]" with a fixed face, which may be far more comfortable, bearing in mind it may not be the face causing the problem, but the rapidly changing expressions.

- Young people often pick up what you are thinking, especially if they have done something wrong. One glance and they know they are in trouble, so words aren't necessary. However, they can get confused if they pick up incongruence: your face saying one thing and your words saying something different.
- If you are overwhelmed by faces you look away for comfort. "If someone doesn't look at you for long enough, you stop looking at them – you mirror their behaviour[66]".

Reading this chapter you will have triggered more energy that you no longer need. I suggest you return to your favourite meditation to release that energy and feel more like you. Just five minutes every day, clearing your energy system and getting into a grounded habit will have a dramatic effect on your overall health.

Chapter 17: The Emotional Roller Coaster

Young people with SpLD and those who care for them will have a whole spectrum of emotions. These may range from being astounded at their skills to being deeply frustrated by their challenges. Their feelings of frustration and their inability to communicate often boil over into extreme anger, producing conflict with other family members. I trust this chapter will explain how and why this happens, as well as giving you new options for combating this tricky situation.

Feeling Emotions and Empathy

Young people with SpLD often struggle with their feelings. For example, autistic people have reduced responses from their mirror neurons, and so find it difficult to "feel the pain of others." To try and deal with this issue, many children in school and at home are taught emotions by rote. Like learning a foreign language, children are instructed to reproduce the appropriate emotional state and actions for any number of different situations.

This is deeply problematic, however. Crucially, such an approach is attempting to assist those who are not in touch with their internal dialogue and feelings. Right and wrong is based on what has been learnt through rules, but what happens if the rule doesn't quite match the situation? You are

flummoxed! Ideally, emotions need to come to you naturally, from inside yourself. To achieve this, however, you must be fully grounded. Empathy or any form of social interaction will never be fluent unless the person can *feel* it. So, if you want to help someone feel their emotions, don't start until they are firmly grounded. In that way, any unwanted emotions can be released (as we've already discussed). Clearing energy from around the heart will allow individuals to develop their own emotions, rather than having them taught by rote. (See simple skill #23)

Empathy is a mixed blessing and something that challenges many. Empathy is to feel someone else's pain, entering into another person's feelings. For instance, if you cry when someone else is upset, you are being empathetic. In my experience as a coach, however, total empathy is not necessarily a great strategy for dealing with SpLD issues. Whilst you want to understand someone's challenge from their perspective, you shouldn't attempt to "feel their pain," as this will compromise your own health. If you were to do so, you would be taking on their energy of pain and feeling it, in just the same way they do.

This situation is avoidable, though. To avoid taking on other people's energy, imagine a lightning rod between you and them, and see their energy just caught on the lightning rod and sent down into the ground.

Allergies and Food Intolerances

A large proportion of the young people with SpLD have allergies and intolerances. Most intolerances are to things you find in your every day environment and diet. In many instances, in fact, these are often the things we crave most. In my experience, the reaction goes back to a time when you were scared or frightened and had those particular substances in or around your system. Your reaction to the fright then gets anchored in those substances, and will eventually develop into an intolerance or allergy. In the future, any re-engagement with such things creates the same reaction (say fear) that, over time, will magnify into panic attacks and the like.

The way I look at allergies and food intolerances is simple; as an abnormal response to a food, drug or something else in the environment that for most people does not cause any symptoms. In short, the body is trying to protect us and may generate a limited or very severe reaction. I see many people who, for instance, love dogs but have an allergic reaction to them. This immediately shows an incongruence within them caused an internal conflict, such as the notion that "part of me loves dogs, but another part really doesn't like to be near them."

If you really want to change this situation, the initial reaction – the point where the energy is lit up – is in fact a great opportunity to start addressing the problem. At the first sign of a reaction, you should attempt to get grounded and start releasing the energy. If you choose to work on an intolerance, work up to it gradually. Start by thinking about next door's cat, for example, and pay careful attention to your experience of these thoughts. At the first sign of discomfort, get grounded and release the energy. Then move on to a picture of a cat, for instance. At the first sign of a negative reaction, repeat the process until you can feel comfortable with any dog or cat. This process is of course meant to be complementary and should not be fully substituted for any prescribed medical solutions.

You can run the same type of process with any intolerance and many of the allergies. Try it for yourself and see! It is all about rebalancing your energy whilst the offending substance is in your energy system. The sooner you can do it after developing an intolerance the better, before it generalises into other areas.

Simple skill #22: Meltdowns

Meltdowns are another aspect of being overwhelmed and scared. Simple things can set people off with a reaction totally out of proportion to the event. This is very similar to an intolerance or allergy, but instead of being to something external you are reacting to something internally generated. This happens because something triggers you to recall, perhaps not even consciously, a previously bad experience. Many people will know how things like frustration with yourself and people making a mess can really "press your buttons." These are very frequent, but not everyone does them. Those with SpLD will have a more violent reaction to minor things such as:

- Plans changing.
- Texture of breakfast cereal.
- Noise of crumpled paper. In the book *House Rules*[67], a principal character (with Asperger's) stated that "he felt as if his internal organs were being crumpled".
- Bright light.
- Things being out of order.

Simply put, you don't need to find out how you came about these associations. Rather, you just need to gain the skills necessary to release them. It isn't about the actual event; rather, the issue is the emotional reaction to the event that your body generates. For those who do not have a great understanding of their emotions, this must be terrifying. Indeed, you may be able to detect the trigger in someone else quite easily, as it may just be a word, a phrase or an attitude that sets off the reaction. The energy won't be yours in present time so you may feel very uncomfortable and it will probably un-ground you. Practise the tools in this book so that you can recall them in seconds when you need them. Once you know the key, you can even practise on an imaginary meltdown, as this will start the process. Meltdowns cause you to spiral out of control, so put in place a routine, for yourself and your child, such as:

✓ **Learn to spot the first sign, before it becomes overwhelming and a full scale meltdown.**
✓ **Get grounded and try to let the mounting energy down into the ground.**
✓ **Use the lake and the magnet to release the energy and clear blocks, or put them in a recycling bin and press the delete button.**
✓ **Some people like the metaphor of re-booting your computer; this will help remind the person that everything is going to be OK, and perhaps even validate themselves. A repetitive familiar task or your own special song may help you too.**
✓ **Imagine a golden ball of healing energy over your head. Let it recover any energy you have left with different people or in different places, clean it up and let it gently filter back into the top of your head, making sure that any energy that is not yours just drifts down into the ground.**

Parents can even imagine this happening for young children. As they grow, teach them the routine for themselves so they can choose to

use it whenever they want, without the need for parents to be around. In addition, you may want to continue using it yourself.

Many therapists use supervision to help them think through an experience with a client, recognising that someone's emotions can have an effect on the observer too. For parents, teachers and family members this is not available, so protect yourself by not sitting right in front of them, keep grounded and imagine lightning rods between you to capture the energy. We need to take care of the carers just as much as the clients.

Simple skills #23: Energy Wash and Recovery

I want to give you a routine for a thorough wash of your complete energetic body, which is great to use from time to time, especially when you have been particularly challenged, a bit like coming home and having a shower after a hard day at the office.

✓ **Sit comfortably with both feet in contact with the floor.**
✓ **Relax and enjoy the sensation of your breath entering and leaving your body.**
✓ **Imagine a beautiful cloud of healing energies is beginning to form above your head and there are three types of energies in it – energies that clear, energies that heal and energies that enhance. And similar energies are forming in the earth below you, energies that are clear, healing and enhancing.**

✓ I invite you to let your inner wisdom and spirit take charge of this and allow your inner wisdom and spirit to start pulling those energies into your space. Give permission for the energy to come into your body and the energy field around your body, clearing, healing and enhancing you and strengthening your connection with your inner wisdom, spirit and wellness. And imagine, as these energies come into your space, that your energy field starts to glow.

✓ Since your energy field is in you and surrounds you, imagine then, the energy clearing the space above your head. There are very important energy centres above your head, so imagine these energies clearing, healing and enhancing the area about three metres (nine feet) above your head all the way down to the top of your head. And let these clearing, healing and enhancing energies remove anybody else's energy from this space, to access more of your own inner wisdom and spirit.

✓ Now let these energies clear the inside of your head including your brain. There is an energy centre in the middle of your head. Imagine all the energy centres in and around your head being cleared, healed, balanced and enhanced.

✓ Now very gently let the energies clear your eyes, your optic nerves, their connection to your brain and the energy (telepathic) channels that flow around your eyes and then over the top of your head down to your neck – clearing, healing, balancing and enhancing.

✓ Now let these energies clear, heal, balance and enhance your ears, inner ears and the channels around them. Now let the energies move down into your nose, mouth and all the channels around them. And as these are being cleared, let them be filled up with healing, balancing and enhancing energies guided by your inner wisdom and spirit.

✓ Now let the energies move down into your throat. There is a major energy centre at the base of the throat, which is all about how we express ourselves in the world. This is often blocked when we have SpLDs. Let these be cleared, healed, balanced and enhanced.

✓ Now let the energies move down into your neck, shoulders arms, hands and fingers – hands and fingers have a lot to do with what we create in this world and how you can have more return on the effort you make.

✓ Now let the energies move down into your heart energy centre and let them dissolve any beliefs around not being good enough, not deserving and not being lovable. Let the energies clear, heal, balance and enhance your heart centre and your entire blood circulatory system. And open this area up to allow yourself to increase your ability to receive. Feel yourself able to breathe gently into and out of your heart. Then feel the positive energies of gratitude, care, appreciation and love radiating from your heart. And open up your heart to receive more validation, gratitude, love and appreciation.

✓ Now let the energies swirl around your chest – the energy centres in your chest are about allowing yourself to be more powerful in your own life. Feel those energies clearing, healing, balancing and enhancing these energy centres. You can even imagine swallowing little balls of this energy and letting them dance around in your lungs, cleaning and clearing all the little intricacies of your whole breathing system.

✓ Now let the energies move into the rest of your abdomen, pelvic area, internal organs, clearing, healing and enhancing.

✓ Now let the energies focus on your internal organs, your nervous system, muscles, tendons and any other specific part of you which needs clearing, healing and enhancing.

✓ In the case of any physical challenges like Dyspraxia, set the very clear intention that any energy channels restricting movement will he cleared, healed, balanced and enhanced and any broken bones will heal to be strong and healthy. Imagine in your mind's eye how bones will look and feel. You may even like to imagine a metaphor to connect the break together, like tiny little threads that build into very strong connections. Use whatever pictures your own inner wisdom wants to show you. Then imagine the energies clearing, healing and enhancing the affected areas and just notice what changes occur under the control of your inner wisdom.

✓ Now you may not know what your immune system looks like, so just imagine a symbol in front of you that represents your immune system, perhaps a rose, a star, whatever suits you. Just watch your immune system as these energies clear, heal and enhance. If your immune system is working very hard at the moment, just watch the symbol as it takes on all the wellness healing.

✓ Similarly you can put up a symbol for your lymph system which is responsible for cleaning out any debris for your body as you return to wellness, so you may even like to imagine some little vacuum cleaners to help. See the clearing, healing and enhancing energies changing that symbol and feel it clearing, healing, enhancing your entire lymph system.

✓ Now let the energies focus on your legs and feet where there are powerful energy centres. These have to do with how you move in the world, let them be set for moving elegantly, confidently, enjoyably and with fun. Feel these being cleared, healed and enhanced.

✓ Now let these energies go down to the part of your energy field below your feet, clearing, healing and enhancing. These energy centres have to do with how you are in the physical world, how you connect with and transform the loving and supportive earth energies.

✓ Now let the energies move into the area in front of you, clearing, healing and enhancing. Now the area behind you. Now travel down each side of you.

✓ Now let the energies clear your entire energy field around you.

✓ When you have finished just enjoy the sensation and notice what it feels like to have your complete energy system cleared.

So now you have your entire energy system glowing and sparkling with wellness. Notice what that feels like as the energy of wellness runs through your body. Stay in that place and enjoy it for as long as you like.

For Young Children

A ten year old child I was helping with her literacy told me that she had a friend in her class who had Asperger's and she always knew when he was "going off on one" and she could help. I was intrigued and asked her more. She gave me an example from a few days before. He was sitting at his desk with a blue card in his hands and she just knew it was bad. She said "What's the matter, Tommy?" and he threw the card at her, saying "Report". She recognised a report card that was given out in school when you had done something wrong. She said, "Never mind, it's not too bad so let's imagine that we can tear it up into squares. Now, think of folding each square into a blue butterfly and let them fly away. Then all you have to do is hand in your work, without getting upset". As if by magic he recovered from his partial meltdown, because the energy had gone, and went to get his school bag. I learn so much listening to my clients and never cease to be impressed with their wisdom, even at such a young age.

George: The past: "Since I was very young, about seven years old, I have been bullied by a number of different people, some of them throughout my entire life. This wouldn't usually be physical bullying, more psychological by isolating me from people and manipulating others into disliking me. I lost confidence in both meeting new people and trying new activities. I always felt I was not good enough. I am often looked on as a 'loner'. When I try to talk to somebody, even if it is someone I have spoken to before, my inner voice tells me that they are going to laugh and mock me. So I usually leave. I have realised that I have been recalling very old memories of events that have held me back all my life. It is no different to learning useful lessons like 'don't touch the stove' - I get the same voice in my head issuing a warning about talking to somebody. This has also affected my confidence in my new favourite sport 'Tricking[68]', which is similar to gymnastics, but doesn't have a set routine. When trying a new move or even ones I have done hundreds of times, all I can think is "you're not good enough - just give up - you'll never be as good as them". This made me slow at learning because it took half my time to fight the thoughts. Although some people do say that I am quite talented at this, I still personally feel and tell myself I am not.

The change: Through coaching, I found that "looking up" prevented me from hearing that inner voice. It gave me back some of the confidence needed to deal with the problems. I also learnt that it is easier to read books when holding them up so that I am looking forward rather than looking down at a table. This made it much more enjoyable for me to read and I could remember what I had read better. Whenever I had looked down and tried to read, I just felt sad. I learnt to memorise and visualise new words I come across, and, because I have a good imagination, I would be able to see the words when I close my eyes. This helped with my school work because I used to be horrible at spelling; I am now starting to remember the correct words and how to spell them.

The present: I am now nearly eighteen. The coaching helped my confidence talking to others without feeling the need to run away. Increased confidence has dramatically helped my "Tricking". I am now learning at a much faster rate and I am enjoying it a lot more. The advice on reading has made me willing to read my first book, the 2nd in the Harry Potter[69] series, which I thought I would probably never try as I disliked reading too much."

This story all represents such an exceptional achievement for George personally that I wanted to include it here and as a postscript...

The results: 3 good A levels and a place on an excellent apprenticeship programme. What a result!

Chapter 18: Other Sensory Skills

This chapter includes some additional tips for those who have more severe SpLDs. They all relate to your sensory system; your imagination (ability to create new pictures), your internal dialogue, your feelings and your auditory skills for speech. It is well worth checking whether these manifest in your young people.

Simple skills #24: But I Haven't Got an Imagination!

You need the ability to create imaginary pictures for all manner of things; for example, following a map, creating imaginary pictures, redecorating a room. Some people really believe they have no imagination and you need to be careful about what imagination means to them – picturing, imagining, recalling, visualising – what words do they use and what do they mean to them? In addition, people may be much better at picturing something than drawing it. To have a good imagination, however, there's no need to be good at Art.

It is important to realise that those who struggle with imagining something they have never seen before often have an extraordinary skill for recalling things they *have* seen. This is often the case with autistic young people, who seem very frightened, making up pictures of something they have never seen. This fact has led me to think about how an individual might goes about, making up a new picture. It may be that being overloaded with *too much* visual recall can crowd out your abilities to make up pictures. Autistic children may have more challenges because of the need to be able to generalise. An example would be if you ask an autistic young person to imagine a

new bedroom. This can be very frightening.

All is not lost, however. Armed with this information, you can help someone construct things they have never seen from familiar parts. Try visualising a large red bus, with an elephant on top, playing a trumpet. Because all the separate elements are known, constructing the new picture may be easier.

Notice whereabouts your images are when you are visualising – your mental geography. To see images in your mind's eye you will most likely be looking up. Now notice whether the image is to your left or right. It maybe one place for pictures, another for letters, yet another for numbers. Most people will visualise things they have seen before in the same place – pictures or words are usually visualised up and slightly to the left. But it *is* a matter of personal choice. When they come to work out a sum, they may do the calculation somewhere else, perhaps up and to the right. When you are constructing a new picture, you may do that in a similar place to the sum, because you are creating something new. You need to help young people work out the best and most effective mental geography for them.

Another trick that works well is to get a young person to imagine Mum's car in their mind's eye and notice where their gaze settles. Get them to imagine driving it to the opposite side, say moving the car from your left to the right. As it goes, it passes through a paint spray and gradually turns pink (or whatever their favourite colour is). Hey presto, you have an imaginary car. You can run the same game and make it even more inventive and imaginative, building up the young person's confidence.

Many parents help their children by making up or finding a picture of a new experience they will have, say, going to a new school. Young people seem to be genuinely frightened of something like a new school. Considering they probably know every inch of their current school, it's really not surprising they are alarmed by something new for which they have no pictures. Chaos often breaks out with changes in routine, because what is about to happen does not fit with their picture of a regular, known activity. I have heard it described as tension sweeping thought their muscles, with the feeling of anxiety increasing rapidly. Changing the direction of that energy into the ground can be really helpful.

Another way you can help your child is for you to imagine the new experience yourself. As mentioned above, children with exceptional visual skills often seem to know exactly what an adult is thinking. Therefore, when you next have to change your plans or go to a new place, get a good image of it yourself and see if this helps your child.

In my opinion, this stress over creating a visual picture is fundamental to so many autistic traits and is driven by a need for visual security. This can manifest itself in many ways. For example:

- Eating by colours/days of the week.
- Clothes in strict colour order.
- Being upset by changing routines.

- Concentration on details.
- Routines and rules.

Simple Skills #25: Developing an Internal Dialogue

Your internal dialogue is that little voice in your head that talks to you. It can give you positive or negative messages as well as check your behaviour, shape your self-concept, keep you safe and acting appropriately. A few examples may be, "I'd better wait for that car to pass before I cross the road", "I need to go to the toilet", "I'd better stop work for dinner now", "I am an idiot", "Don't hit him, you will get into trouble".

Try this one out for yourself. When you are next really busy, there are numerous things flying around in your head and your feet barely touch the floor. Do you feel un-grounded? If so, keep this up for a little while until you have really had enough. Then try walking around. If you feel wobbly, go and sit somewhere quiet and attempt to drop into a more grounded state. Have you suddenly realised you have forgotten to pick up the children, need something to eat or drink or go to the bathroom? This is proof that when you are un-grounded, your internal dialogue is not working well, if at all.

This point is crucial. To even *hear* your internal dialogue you must be grounded. But how do you develop your internal dialogue? Most people develop a sense of what is right and wrong by past events in their lives. In addition, many people receive and absorb a substantial amount of programming from their parents. For instance, Mum will tell you to stop at the kerb and check whether any cars are coming before you cross. She will have do this several times, and over time (hopefully) those events should be coded into your brain, as an internal dialogue – that little voice in your head that keeps you safe, telling you to "wait patiently for a gap in the traffic". If a child is ungrounded, not paying attention or in their own world, however, this valuable information will probably go in one ear and straight out the other. The child will be unable to properly absorb the warnings designed to keep them safe.

The solution to this problem is simple. When you are trying to teach your child, make sure they are grounded or you can almost guarantee what you've said will not be retained. You can suggest they make up pictures in their memory of how they are going to keep safe, just like comprehension.

Another indication of a lack of internal dialogue might be signposted by the child in question often taking things very literally, without any sense check. For many such children, they view the world as being very black and white. Indeed, this situation is often not helped by the English language, with its many expressions that don't mean literally what they  say. For instance: "Take a seat", "Mark my words", "Hang around", "Just a second", "Get off my back", "I am kicking myself", "Don't even breathe".

People with little access to their internal dialogue may make inappropriate, hurtful and spiteful comments. As such, it is invaluable if you can get young people to think for themselves and make their own decisions, even at a very young age. Many young people grow up having made few decisions for themselves. They are told to "do this" and "not to do that", which does not help them develop their own personal sense of what actions are or are not appropriate.

Jimmy was a very active and challenging little boy. He was extremely visual and a little dynamo who wore out everyone around him. At the same time he was highly intelligent and a delight when he was behaving well, which wasn't very often. Exhausting his whole family, he was frequently told to do this and not do that. They had given up on him taking decisions for himself and it took too much time out of their busy schedule to try and make him.

At Christmas, in the nativity play, he noticed that the stage was covered in square tiles. He was just standing there as a shepherd and his mind began to wander, and he imagined these square were a hopscotch line. Without further thought he hop scotched across the stage and back again. You can imagine the consternation. Hopscotch in the middle of a nativity play! Naturally, his parents were called in and told about his inappropriate behaviour. Nobody actually asked him why he had done it and he had little experience of listening to an internal dialogue that might have been trained by taking more decisions.

Speech

Many children with SpLD can have extreme auditory skills; struggling to speak, using alternative voices and maybe talking incessantly. Here are some experiences you may find useful.

It is known that children with Down's Syndrome don't speak until they can see words.[70] Once people start to visualise words, their speech improves. Indeed, I have taught this simple skill to many speech therapists who have gone on to use it for a number of other clients.

One useful tip is to simply continue the conversation when a young person's speech falters, whilst giving them space to collect their thoughts. With a young child, just continue, giving the impression that you have understood them[71]. Building their confidence and self esteem enables them to work out the correct words later.

Some young people develop an alternative voice that they slip into or out of without seeming to notice. It seems that if a child feels unable to explain something, sometimes stepping into the shoes of a fictional character makes it easier. For example, in House Rules[72], Jacob's specialist subject was crime scenes. As such, he would borrow the words and voice of his crime scene investigator hero when he couldn't find his own.

When you first awake, do you notice how sometimes it is difficult to speak? It is like looking for words in alphabet soup! Once you become grounded and "really here", it is much easier. When George VI was really stressed, speech was impossible because he'd become so un-grounded. Rolling him on the ground enabled him to speak, although this obviously wasn't particularly practical!

> In the story about Robert in chapter 11, when he slipped into the character of Mickey Mouse, his mother would notice he was un-grounded. When Mum grounded herself, he got that feeling too and came out of being this character, back into his normal voice.

Simple skills #26: No Feelings

Parents often report that children can't express any feelings for them, can't make eye contact or can't bear to be touched by them. Emotionally this is a truly uncomfortable place for the whole family, leading to feelings of inadequacy, guilt and so on. It is crucial that parents let go of all those emotions and try looking from a different perspective.

When you are un-grounded, being touched can be very uncomfortable. Some people realise that when they are asleep they are extremely un-grounded – this is quite a normal state and enables the mind to travel freely overnight, in and out of dreams. When the child wakes up, they may take a little while to "get back here". However, putting the child's feet out of bed and onto the floor will help them get grounded again. You may encourage the child to imagine their egg-timer pouring energy back into their body. If the child is touched in this un-grounded state, it can feel like an electric shock and will undoubtedly be very uncomfortable.

If you have a child who doesn't like to be touched, check whether this is always so and notice whether they are grounded. By suggesting a child becomes grounded before you touch them, you may find you get a much better reaction. You could also just think about your own 'I'm a bad parent' emotions and realise their reaction was not to you, but to their own state. This will help you get rid of these negative thoughts. This sensitivity when un-grounded may also account for why autistic children often hate tags in clothing; tags will really hurt their skin when you are ungrounded. Dr. Cheri Florance often commented on her son's lack of emotions and on the occasion he caught his hand in the car door, saying that there was very little reaction from him, he had possibly become completely disconnected from his body.

Chapter 19: Prevention and "Recipes" for SpLDs

This chapter gives you a summary of how you may prevent very young children developing symptoms of SpLDs. For those who have developed the symptoms, you will find recipes to help you focus on where to start. Again these recommendations are born out of what has worked for others, to which you can add your own experiences.

Prevention

Whenever I work with young people or adults who are underachieving or with diagnoses of SpLD, I am always concerned about how this experience can help with prevention for others. For me, the central question is: "what skills could we teach people young enough to stop this train of destruction in the first place?" Furthermore, could these symptoms have been prevented? If so, how could that have been achieved?

In this book you will have seen how some SpLDs are an unconscious competence – a learnt behaviour. Sometimes you are clearly not born with a challenge; in other instances, however, a person develops the traits over time. I have not seen any evidence that you are born with Dyslexia or Dyscalculia. In fact the story about William, in chapter 11, chronicles a journey into developing Dyslexia, and Nuala Gardner reports in *A Friend like Henry*[73] that after years of experience with her first autistic child, her second child developed normally and then autistic traits appeared later.

As young people grow up with SpLDs, feeling disconnected from others and isolated, they find it more difficult to change their experience. But with the right teacher it is never too late; my oldest client to date was eighty-five. It is like divergent roads; the young people who are 1% adrift from their peers at age four, may be 30% adrift by the time they are teenagers and worse still as adults.

As such, it is vital that we focus on *prevention*. The issue with prevention is, of course, that you don't know whether or not a particular individual would eventually have developed the challenge. In large part, you can only refer to a statistical probability. Prevention is a difficult topic; think how people blissfully ignore the dire warnings on every cigarette packet sold in the UK. In large part, all we can do is to make people aware of what may happen and suggest that they attempt to understand their own experience. From there, people will hopefully be able to make decisions based on their own inner wisdom, and not on other people's view of them.

For parents of young children, it is often very difficult to deal with issues and problems in a relaxed manner. As such, it is very common for adults dealing with difficult and stressful situations to be overly emotional and thus become un-grounded. As I have pointed out before, *being un-grounded is contagious!* The more grounded you stay, seeing past the current problem with curiosity, the more your family will too. Please don't blame yourself; the very fact that you worry about being a good mum or dad should tell you that you already are one!

Very young children learn through play, so we can start with finding very simple games that will encourage them to develop the following "natural skills":

- Recalling static letters and words (for literacy) – start with Post-Its stuck on familiar objects, for example "bricks" written on toy bricks, "table" on the table, "chair" on the chair and so on all around the house. There is no need to make a big effort as young people will soon start associating words with objects and remembering words as internal visual images.
- Encourage children to enjoy books. You can start reading to them from just a few weeks old; they will enjoy the peacefulness and personal contact. The more vivid you can make the story, the better they will be able to visualise. As they grow older, keep reading to them more advanced books that you don't expect them to read. This gives them the opportunity to visualise. Books without pictures are generally written in more creative text to stimulate visualisation.
- Recalling logos – these are all around us and are actually pictures – logos on chocolate bars, breakfast cereal boxes, construction toys, etc. Any of these will help a young person recall a visual image.
- Recalling pictures of familiar objects – cover objects on a tray and try remembering what they are.
- Controlling whether they are recalling a movie or still pictures. Ask them about the pictures they are visualising – try the game of statues to get the child to visualise a still picture.
- Visualising how a specific letter or word is formed. If they watch you, they can create a movie in their memory and try for themselves,

either in the air or on paper. (Make sure you are sitting next to them rather than in front of them so the letter or word you are writing is the right way around).

- Visualising an abacus or number bonds to help them with addition, progressing to static numbers for mental maths.
- Being able to copy down without looking at the paper. Once a child can hold a pencil they can develop this skill, without even understanding the content. (See chapter 14).
- Creating imaginary pictures – start constructing them from bits you already know, e.g. an elephant, sitting on top of a bus, driving down the high street in town.
- Converting stories into picture memories (essential for comprehension). Encourage them to make up pictures when you are reading to them, one sentence at a time to start with.
- Converting lists into picture memories (short term memory) – there are many techniques used by memory systems
- Improving grounding and reducing stress (essential for concentration) – ground yourself first; then teach them to ground their environment for themselves.
- Making up imaginary stories (for story writing) – see below.

It is very useful for both you and your young person to be able to make up imaginary stories. Think of an object such as an elephant and ask your creative side to start playing a movie about the elephant. Just say what you are seeing. What happens next? Maybe your elephant is walking in the jungle, or maybe it is carrying logs. Whatever it does is right for you and you could easily tell the story just by describing the pictures you see. It is a simple skill and young children really love their parents to make up their own personal imaginary stories and an invaluable skill if parents struggle to read aloud. Now ask small children to try it. You'll find they may be able to tell you very long stories, once they realise how easy it is. As the child grows up, actively encourage them to make up their own stories for creative writing.

Specific Diagnoses – The Recipes to Start With

This section uses the SpLD labels to help the reader determine exactly where to start for themselves or their child/children.

Against each label is a brief summary of symptoms which you can observe. Indicated are some of the reasons we have found for these and the appropriate skills to overcome them. The lists are not intended to be exhaustive, but they will give you a good start and an opportunity to add in your personal recommendations. They are tools to help individuals, families and teachers learn more about their own experience and that of others.

First take a look at this wheel again, you will be able to notice which areas are most relevant to the young person with SpLD you are assisting. Of course, every case is different and you may notice significant differences for specific individuals. Dyslexia is, for example, 70% sensory control, 15% grounding, 10% family involvement, 5% energy blocks. For a person with Dyspraxia it may look like 70% energy blocks, 20% grounding and 10% family connections. For Autism, grounding is likely to be a dominant factor at 85%, "super visual" say 10% and perhaps 5% family and it is difficult to see anything else until progress is made on these.

Remember to look past the symptoms to their exceptional talents. Understanding these talents you will find ways to teach visual people visually. Any parent is capable of helping their child in this way, and once you start to understand how they see the world, you can work out how they can learn any specific topic visually. *They* are the ones with the exceptional visual talents – you will get the best results if *they* work out answers which work best for their visual brain. It certainly doesn't matter if your visual skills are not as good as those of your child. Indeed, this is often the case.

By keeping an open mind you can see occasions when an individual has debilitating symptoms and times when they don't. So at some level they know how to change and how to do it. It is a question of capturing those gems, which take an individual to a much more empowering place.

In my experience, these young people are very bright, albeit in ways not measurable by current intelligence standards and tests. When you can involve the whole family and school unit, progress for all is far more successful. Naturally, the earlier these skills are learned, the better. The later you leave it, the more confused people become.

ADHD :

What we notice: hyperactivity; no focus; lack of concentration; inability to sit still; very talkative; concentrating on multiple screens at once; repetitive thought patterns; e.g. rehearsal and no deletions.

Known challenges: when trying to visualise an object, thousands may be seen, possibly all moving and too close. With this happening, concentration is impossible.

Skills to learn: grounding; validation; control over visual pictures, sequencing. If wound like a coiled spring, releasing energy into the ground, (feet flat on floor, even better with no shoes and on the grass). Improve concentration by visualising static images. Eliminate unwanted images and concentrate on just one.

The most important point is grounding – taking focus out of your head and into your body, a skill with which any sportsman is familiar. If you aren't grounded you will be wobbly and concentration will be impossible. You will probably need to clear blocks so you are comfortable when grounded. One adult client saw 250 birds when un-grounded, 2 when grounded.

The second point to check is visual memory. Here, ensuring pictures are static is essential because being stuck in movies is confusing and ruins reading and spelling abilities. This is common for those young people who are great on a computer games and used to images going even faster than reality. They may have multiple videos running (the more stress, the more videos) and they need to learn to turn off those images which don't require their immediate attention.

The third point is to get all those thought processes under control through grounding, enabling focus and concentration.

Dyslexia or Poor Literacy:

What we notice: frustration; anger; disconnection from reading and school work; poor spelling; poor reading; disorganisation, struggling with high frequency words, letter reversals when very young, panicking about words that are not understood – sometimes resorting to head banging to stop or distract from the panic, very bright children who inexplicably find literacy very difficult, reading often better than spelling, difficulty in copying – often able to manage only one letter at a time, poor punctuation, science formulas moving around in the mind's eye

Known challenges: not visualising words; words moving; auditory impairment; un-grounded.

Skills to learn: visualising words (even for the visually impaired); grounding to keep the images still.

Dyscalculia or Poor Numeracy:

What we notice: frustration; anger; disconnection from maths; phobic about numbers.

Known challenges: inability to visualise numbers; numbers moving.

Skills to learn: visualise numbers (even for the visually impaired); grounding to keep them still; getting control when working with formulas; learn visually what numbers mean to improve addition and subtraction; visualise number triangles for multiplication and division.

Dyspraxia:

What we notice: being un-grounded causes many symptoms – confusion; slurred speech; unsteadiness; poor handwriting; lack of co-ordination; clumsiness; being in a trance-like state.

Known challenges: open to energy when very young/birth, blocked energy channels; inability to get grounded and hence develops secondary problems. Possible traumatic pregnancy/birth/energy separation from mother.

Skills to learn: clearing energy; grounding; validation; check eye line when walking (you don't want to be looking down in your emotions).

Dysgraphia:

What we notice: poor or dreadful hand-writing.

Known challenges: covers up poor spelling; no visual image of letters; energy blocks hand motor skills.

Skills to learn: visual spelling; copying down from the board; good writing; create and follow a mental image of 'nice' handwriting; clearing energy blocks.

Tourettes:

What we notice: ticks and shouting out.

Known challenges: can be viewed as a pattern breaker for overload; people describe energy moving up through their body and needing to be released. Un-grounded people or those in a very busy environment find it worse.

Skills to learn: how to ground – both the individual and the environment. Redirection of energy as it moves through the body, back down into the ground.

Verbal Dyslexia or Dyspraxia, Slow Speech, Hesitation, Stammering:

What we notice: confused or poor speech; energy blocks; multiple voices; loss of self esteem.

Known challenges: un-grounded, problems selecting or articulating words (Down's syndrome children can't say words until they can visualise them[74], teaching young people to visual words helps speech); perfectionism; stress

Skills to learn: get grounded; visualisation of words; releasing previous trauma; don't correct a very young child when they first speak, let them work out mistakes for themselves (they will)[75].

Asperger's Syndrome

What we notice: multiple voices; taking things literally; meltdowns, upset by incongruence (someone verbalising something which is contradicted by their non-verbal communication – may be lying); difficulty forming relationships; inappropriate behaviour, total expert in one particular field; inability to communicate.

Known challenges: un-grounded (leading to sensory impairment); energy blocked when upset.

Skills to learn: get grounded; releasing previous trauma; grounding the room when overwhelmed; help their imagination to find solutions (e.g. the imaginary cloak for the child that annoys your young person).

Autism

What we notice: locked in their own world; unaware of the wider world; lack of imagination; fear of the future and the unknown; exceptional visual recall; very sensitive to energy; dislike of being touched; lack of eye contact; sensitive to incongruence; human faces creating sensory overload; associated into everything; may overreact to or not notice loud noises; lack of appetite; doesn't get normal toilet signals; feels overloaded; 'plugged into mains'.

Known challenges: very un-grounded (leading to sensory impairment) even at identity level; energy blocked.

Skills to learn: get grounded; release previous trauma, teach visually, including visual construct; enter into an obsession to get engagement; sensory skills; build on fixed faces (Thomas the Tank, dogs); dissociation from unpleasant emotions; work from a visual world (e.g. ask visual questions, sequencing); clearing energy including telepathic channels; development of internal dialogue; keeping your own energy out of their space.

"I have a 7 year old, high functioning autistic son. I removed him from school because of anxiety and he has been home educated for the last 21 months. Using the visual learning techniques has greatly helped our family. My son had such a great fear of reading and writing that we had stopped all reading for a year.

After trying the techniques in short bursts for three weeks, he is able to read, spell, write better and do word searches in double quick time. When doing word searches, he looks for the whole word after visualising it and the word jumps out from the page. He is a very visual child and this system is a dream for him. The phonics system never resonated with him. I'm very excited that he'll be a confident reader by the time he's eight. I thought he would be much older and possibly always have difficulties. I think every child would benefit from learning this system and I hope to see it introduced into schools", Nicky, Hertfordshire

Epilogue: A Cultural Change in Education?

One of the most rewarding aspects of my work is seeing individuals fundamentally change their experiences of learning and education. Another is hearing stories of how they have gone on to teach others. Truly solving the issues surrounding SpLD is much larger than the individual level, however. What society needs is a fundamental cultural change, one that will increase success for all, not just for a few. To consider how this change might be achieved, let's first look at where we are today. From there, we can begin to understand where we would like to be, and what actions can be taken in schools, communities and businesses to improve the current situation.

What is the Situation Today?

A recent Government report published in the UK[76] states that "we are letting our children and young people down," and recommends an overhaul of the system currently in place for SpLD assessment and provision. Though the recommendations are no doubt needed, but the paper's solutions do not fundamentally change the substance of our current educational approach. The report covers the whole range of those who are disabled or identified as having special educational need. This book is about how the education system can challenge "families having to put up with a culture of low expectations about what children with SpLD can achieve at school"[77].

As Andy Burnham[78], one of the authors of the report, puts it, the paper "is a review of the way we support children with Special

Educational Needs (SEN)". In particular, there is no mention of how educational practices could be changed to assist those children who learn *differently*.

The role of teachers has always been to identify and nurture talent. Such educators are in many ways constricted by the current approaches to SpLD, however. The National Curriculum in the UK calls for multi-sensory teaching and learning. However, the stark fact is that very few teachers understand *how* a child learns visually and the mistakes they may make. It is not in their teacher training.

The report also acknowledges the importance of early identification, which is essential and needs to be coupled with a better understanding of how children learn and what can be put in place to help them better use their learning differences. Delays in getting the support they need leads to deterioration in self-esteem, behaviour and mental health. The vital thing is to get away from support being just reactive to problems in the classroom as they emerge. Rather, we must offer the necessary support to help people change and overcome their confusion. We need visual learning skills to be included in mainstream education, coupled with proactive coaching from teachers and parents. These people can become very effective advocates for children, helping them over their confusion at a very young age.

In an article about the report, Dr. Neville Brown says "It is well-known that phonics is not the be-all and end-all of literacy learning[79]". In my experience, this message has not got through to any but a very small percentage of schools in specific counties in the UK. Moreover, this is not a message that has got through to families. At this current time, almost all schools claim that they are instructed to teach phonics and phonics alone. However, some Head teachers open to finding the very best for all their students are following this approach.

In addition, any far-reaching cultural change has to incorporate families, which is much more of a challenge for schools. Although many parents try to help a child feel better with comments like "Don't worry, son, I could never do maths at school and I managed all right", in the long run this is an unhelpful approach. Rather than offering effective encouragement, the young person will come to believe that they can never improve and that there isn't any point in trying. It is generally known in schools that parents and other family members may have similar learning challenges. Schools can promote an integrated approach for all family members through parents' evenings when they explain how they are teaching children to parents. This will allow everyone to benefit!

In January 2011, the first report from the Government's Education Committee said, "Therefore, we encourage the Government to promote language comprehension as well as word recognition and phonics skills throughout the infant curriculum[80]". Word recognition is one element of visual learning and is essential for literacy. I am unable to discover how and when this will be integrated into the strategy in schools. In addition, the Early Years Foundation Stage[81] doesn't even mention learning visually.

One of my concerns about the education system today is the lack of people taking an overview of education from four years of age through to adulthood, considering the personal and financial implications for poor literacy and numeracy both for the individual, their family and employment.

Whenever I teach our bright young people these skills to improve literacy, numeracy, concentration, valuing themselves etc., their families look at me and say, "Why isn't this being taught in schools?" I have no valid answer, except to say that this is my sole mission! We need to drop our pre-occupation with judging what hasn't been done in the past, and instead get on with what can be done really easily, *now!* As Baroness Warnock recently put it, "For good practice, I fear, we still have to look to individuals who are determined to help deprived and disabled children to flourish. Mercifully, they still exist.[82]"

We Need People to Feel Empowered

It is clear that things need to change. We need people engaged in their education, their communities and society. We need our young people to feel empowered to learn by providing them with all the skills they need at an early age. If we accompany this with the large doses of encouragement that they desperately need from adults, we may finally begin to get somewhere.

Though many young people know they "aren't getting it" the way they're currently being taught, instead of leading to questions being asked about the methods used instead leaves the learners feeling stupid. In addition, when they or their parents voice an opinion, they are often ignored. This causes increasing resentment and frustration. Who would want to spend time in school when they are disengaged and confused? For example, I have been told by so many parents that high frequency words are torture for them and their children.

But generally teachers are not curious as to *why* this is the case and, as such, they keep doing things that clearly don't work for many children. To truly empower young people, we need to listen to *them*, as they are the best, most knowledgeable experts on how they learn.

What Would We Have to Do?

You have already started to improve the current situation by reading this book. Start putting the skills into practice now if you have not done so already. Pick those that suit you best and develop your own recipe for change. Wherever you start will be right for you; just trust your own inner wisdom and pick out one or two things to try out, first on yourself and then with your young people. Observe what happens and make necessary changes. Visualising is a fun sport; if you enjoy your learning and have fun, it will be much more successful. You can ask for help if you need it, but the most important thing to do is to take *action*. Continuing to do the things that don't work will only lead to the same results.

As mentioned above, we have astonishingly competent people who would love to improve the system. To live differently involves thinking differently, seeing the world and ourselves from a new perspective. Many children seem to me to be doing just that and yet we label these young people as having SpLD.

Change can only been achieved through collaboration and the desire to move the concept forward. We want the very best for everyone, and that means creating an environment of openness to new ideas. We also need to "let go" of some of our limiting beliefs about what young people can and cannot do.

Individual parents, teachers and schools are already adapting and changing their approach to SpLD, but we are still dearly in need of clear directives throughout the education system that help people understand how people learn visually. From there, we need to encourage forms of teaching that engage every pupil. As mentioned previously, multi-sensory teaching and learning is already in the National Curriculum in the UK and incorporated in learning strategies worldwide.

When you consider how we teach children and how their knowledge is assessed, we spend most of the time teaching them a huge amount of facts, on which children can be more easily tested and assessed. We spend less time teaching them **how to** do things, which is developing their capabilities.

Primary school children will often express creativity through art, yet in the UK we rarely teach them painting or drawing skills until secondary school (eleven years and above) when they start to learn

2D and 3D perspectives. There seems to be an ingrained acceptance that someone is either artistic or not artistic. When teachers in primary school have the capability to teach drawing skills, the results are hugely beneficial. The more we can focus on what young people can do, the faster the challenges drift away.

In addition, teachers are often constricted by both time and class sizes. We accept we need to teach kids how to tie shoe laces, but we also need to focus on teaching them **how to** draw, **how to** create visual images of words and numbers in their mind's eye, **how to** clear their energy system and **how to** easily "let go" of negative emotions. We need to focus on how people who are good at something do it – for example, get a child to watch someone good at drawing, ask them to take a video and then have a go themselves.

The bonus is that this approach could save the education systems around the globe a financial fortune, while at the same time reducing the stress and grief imposed on children, parents, families and schools. We believe that people can achieve amazing things and be resilient as long as they don't drop into the victim mode of "I am stupid, I need someone to fix me". It is not a question of one specific approach being better than another. Rather, any individual needs to develop a combination of several approaches for themselves and for their families.

We are not proving anyone wrong, but rather opening up possibilities and documenting some of the skills others have found useful, so that you can try them for yourself. Once you show your brain how to do something, often through metaphors or mental rehearsal, it is astonishing how quickly it makes the necessary adjustments.

The Education System for Lifelong Learning – from Nursery to Adult Education

The whole education system needs direction to implement this approach. We need children at the centre of our approach to teaching, making sure we engage them in learning in a way they can understand. It is no good giving Local Education Authorities more autonomy if they don't listen to their own pupils, let alone experts in the field.

The way to make substantial change in any system is to change the cause and then manage the symptoms. So, we need to get the teachers in infant years (four to seven years old) properly integrating visual learning into their classes, whilst helping the older ones with individual and group intervention. We also need to engage the parents at every opportunity, making the learning easy enough that they can teach others.

Schools are doing their best to implement the directions they have been given but they are short of funds and resources. In addition, they are often extremely stressed and overwhelmed by changing priorities outside of their control. I do feel that the teachers, who have vast practical experience in education, can integrate these simple tools into their classrooms for the best possible effect.

Crucially, primary schooling is the key age for effecting preventative change for SpLDs. By starting early, we can intervene before confusion becomes overwhelming and help prevent positive by-products from emerging. Once you get into a seeing learning from the point of view of our young people, you can work out how to teach almost anything visually. Visual is a young person's specialist subject, so let's help them use it to their best advantage.

Teacher training and Continuous Professional Development (CPD) must be extended to educate teachers in how people learn visually. Visual learning has the added benefit of increasing engagement and reduces confusion in the classroom. This book is a great place to start and I hope to see it in reading lists for teacher training. For those teachers who are not great at literacy themselves, this really offers a double benefit – their literacy skills will improve and they will become the best teachers for SpLD, as they will really understand what had been missing all their lives. The book will also be available on CD, for those who are short of time. The principles could easily be put into every teacher training programme in just a couple of hours.

When young people change schools or go to college, it is a great opportunity to check out their "natural skills" and help them to use them most effectively. With the increasing numbers of young people diagnosed with an SpLD (let alone those who just have poor literacy, numeracy and concentration), a few hours remedial work when they enter a new environment may be worth days, months and years of frustration, underachievement and support from Learning Assistants.

In business there is a huge reluctance amongst employees to disclose what they believe to be personal deficits of SpLDs, which trigger such bad memories of failure and even humiliation at school. Businesses can really make a contribution here by offering their staff assistance to overcome difficulties with new skills; we know these people are intelligent with some exceptional gifts. This will improve the efficiency of the business and, secondly, enable a parent to teach their own children, hence breaking the cycle of family confusion. There are certain times when adults will be more open to this change: when applying for that first job, preparing for exams, when looking for a new job, when having their first child or when going for a promotion. You will find that added motivation is invaluable.

Charities have done a great job supporting people with SpLD and now they are ideally situated to promote a coaching paradigm. Instead of being known for supporting people with SpLD, I am sure they would rather be positioned in the vanguard of positive change.

A New Perspective – Just Imagine

Now that you have been introduced to the key concepts in this book, please consider what it would be like if we took a different perspective? Imagining how it could be will free up your mind to start manifesting change in your environment. These are my initial thoughts, please create your own.

Everyone with or without SpLDs has within them the capabilities to succeed. It is inbuilt within them! Learning, to me, is more about learning how to do something, rather than just learning content – stuff. We learn skills by experience – you can learn how to ride a bike, draw a picture, score a goal, but until you try it out for yourself, you aren't likely to be very successful. We learn some skills naturally and with others we need a bit of help. If the learning process doesn't work, we may need help to understand where we are going wrong. It is here that the role of a coach can help us change that experience – this is the role of a coach. If one person can do something, we can teach others to do the same thing, once we understand how they do it.

I have difficulty spotting the difference between gifted people and those with SpLD. If every day we looked past the deficits of someone's behaviour to their exceptional talents, the world of SpLD would change and we would see their gifts. In addition some have much to teach us about their exceptional skills.

When we know something works, it is our responsibility as adults to offer it to others. Just imagine everyone has a strong visual memory, like an imaginary whiteboard where they recall pictures, words, numbers and revision notes on anything they want to learn. Imagine they can wipe it clean whenever they like, perform calculations and imagine new pictures that they have never seen before. It has an infinite capacity, is always with you and will never let you down.

This approach will, I believe, empower our young people to be the exceptional human beings they came here to be.

Appendix A: Learning to Visualise

Visualisation, a key tool of the intuitive mind, involves seeing pictures as though projected on a screen. The screen may be inside the head of the individual or just a few feet in front of them. Visualisation is a key element to visual thinking.

Humans have the skill to visualise. Almost everyone recognises their parents at just a few weeks old and, if a parent were to don a wig or hat, the child would probably cry. So we know, even at this very young age, they are matching the picture in their memory to what they see in front of them.

For most people these images go on all the time; young people often enjoy these images yet they can become overwhelming. This happens if they are moving rapidly – at similar speed to a computer game. Or they may appear as multiple images – similar to watching many screens in a TV store. The images may evoke scary memories or be appearing too close to the eyes of the individual. The skill of tuning up the visual field can be learnt quickly and this puts the individual back in control.

If you don't think you are a visual person, you may be struggling to hold onto images for long enough. They may appear in a flash so you recognise what they are and can't hold on to the image.

For example, think of your car or your parents' car and you will know what colour it is. Some people will have a perfect picture of the car. However, don't get into "picture envy" – you may have a perfect photo-like picture, a black and white shot, a cartoon or you may just know what it looks like – whichever you have is perfect for you. Alternatively you can "just pretend," and for different images you will find you have different experiences. Think of your favourite sports team, for example, exactly what they are wearing when competing? You will soon realise you <u>can</u> recall pictures.

Formation of visual images can be helped, however, by looking up to your inner screen. Your mind's eye is located between and slightly above your eyebrows. The act of raising your eyes triggers the visual part of your brain. This is useful because it helps you enter a relaxed state in which to picture things. If you do this with your eyes closed, it may enhance the images you want to access.

Struggling to visualise is counterproductive. The more you relax and withdraw from the sensory input of the world, the more easily images will form.

To begin, choose a place free from distractions and switch off your phone. There is nothing more irritating than an image beginning to form and then being shattered by a disturbance. I often find that images start to appear and then it is as if you can look deeper into them and they develop more detail.

Do not assume you're doing something wrong because the instruction says differently. It's your intuition you are accessing so work with what you get; it is an excellent sign that your intuition is communicating with you.

To prove to yourself that you can use your mind's eye for visualisation, ask a friend to read this list to you, slowly at first and then progressively getting faster:

✓ **A bright red ball > A bright yellow square > An orange triangle > A table > A chair > A table and chairs > Your childhood home > Your first school > Your desk > Your teacher > Your child > Your partner > Your mother > Your great-great grandmother > Your grand child > Your least favourite place > The surface of Mars > the centre of the earth.**

Very few people find this impossible - a bit challenging in places perhaps but the imagination will fill in the gaps. In visualisation, active imagination acts as a vehicle for intuition.

Notice, too, whether your other senses come into play. Do you smell your least favourite place – does your nose wrinkle with distaste?

I want you now to set up the best quality pictures possible by tuning up your mental geography. Did you notice where the pictures were? Whether they were still or moving? Were they very close or too far away? How was their brightness and clarity? Think about tuning in a TV, you need to achieve:

- still images, for example, like taking a freeze frame from a video
- clear pictures – imagine changing the brightness and focus
- the pictures need to be about three to five feet away, to the right or left, not too close nor too far away
- if they are too small, imagine increasing their size, as you would increase the size of a picture on a computer.

Some very visual individuals may find it hard to keep the pictures still, either being stuck in videos running very fast, the images being too far away or the pictures flashing up for too short a time to be any use. Relax, take a couple of deep breaths and imagine you are a tree with deep roots down into the ground. They go all the way to the centre of the earth and spread out all around. You are centred, so nobody can knock you over. Now you will find you have better control over your pictures and can get them to stay still.

Go back to the last exercise and check out your experience again, making all the adjustments you can for your own comfort. Don't worry if this doesn't happen immediately, a little practice will bring great rewards; you are just tuning up your mental geography to be the best it can for you and with a little practice it will improve.

For the next exercise I would like you to get more specific.

✓ **Eating an Apple: Sit comfortably. Now imagine that you are holding ripe green, juicy apple in your left hand. Feel its weight, coolness and smooth roundness. In your right hand you hold a knife. Peel the top of the apple.**
✓ **Then cut yourself a slice. You will feel the juice oozing out and smell the aroma of freshly peeled apple. As you take a bite, you realise it is a cooking apple, it is very sour and sharp.**

Appendix B: Background to Earthing and Grounding

If you are reading this, you are here on the planet, so being firmly connected is a natural place to be. "Most people know standard electronic equipment needs a stable ground to function well. So too, the body needs a stable grounding to function well. Every living thing draws energy from the earth whether through feet, paws, hooves or roots.[83]"

The sole (or plantar surface) of your foot has some 1300 nerve endings per square inch. Several of our body's energy channels which penetrate major organs of the body are found in the feet and toes. So to ensure we can access the earth's energy, it is essential to connect. Eunice Ingham, the "mother of modern Reflexology," states: "The nerves in our body may be likened to an electrical system. It will be our ability to make normal contact with the electricity in the ground, through our feet and from the elements or atmosphere surrounding us, which will determine the degree of power we are able to manifest in the proper functioning of your system. Trying to get normal contact, when there is congestion in these nerve terminals in the feet, is like trying to put a plug into a defective socket."

"Have you ever noticed a subtle tingling or sensation of warmth rising from your feet during a barefoot stroll on a sandy beach or a field glistening with dew? Did you feel revitalised at the end of your walk? If you did, you experienced the earth energising your body[84]". There is a vital continuum between the earth and the living organisms that dwell on it, the earth is a living complex organism with very nourishing and mothering qualities, hence the term "Mother Earth." It has the ability to comfort and balance.

Connecting equipment and appliances to the earth is known as earthing or grounding. It protects equipment against shocks, shorts and interference. Those who work with electronic components will be familiar with earthing straps to save people shorting electronic components. Applied to people, earthing naturally protects the body's delicate bioelectrical circuitry against static electrical changes and interference. Most importantly it facilitates the reception of free electrons and a host of energies from "Mother Earth."

David Wolfe, authority on health and lifestyle, names "the common shoe" as perhaps "the world's most dangerous invention". After fifteen years of nutritional and lifestyle research, he incriminates the shoe as one of the "most destructive culprits of inflammation and autoimmune illnesses[85]". Modern day high heels are even more

extreme with very little of the shoe even in contact with the ground. We even have metaphoric expressions like "my feet haven't touched the ground," to describe a very busy lifestyle. Some people will admit that they realise they can think better with their shoes off. Autistic young people often throw off their shoes at home. They intuitively know that this helps them, providing a better awareness of the position of their body – their proprioception sense. Even breaking your arm is enough to upset your proprioception sense. Some people say "It's the only way to feel as if I am really here".

Electricians working with live electricity protect themselves against a shock by wearing rubber soled shoes or by standing on a rubber mat which insulates them from the earth. In our cities, look at the amount of concrete and tarmac and the number of high rise buildings we have and you'll start to realise how difficult it is for many people to be or feel grounded. Like the electrician, there is a barrier between them and the earth. There are ways around this which we will come to, but nothing replaces direct contact with the earth.

In our modern environment we are constantly bombarded with free radicals; excessive amounts are caused by stress, diet, the environment, etc. Free radicals, circulating within our body and energy system, look for negatively charged electrons and will destroy good cells to access those electrons. Antioxidants have a great supply of negatively charged electrons, which serve to neutralise the free radicals, preventing some of the damage free radicals might otherwise cause.

The ground provides the biggest and best supply of natural electrons that exists. Wearing shoes or spending time in a concrete inner city, insulates us from earth energy and this supply. There has been a recent study from the University of Illinois[86] on how green play settings reduce ADHD symptoms. Think of a container with the air sucked out of it. The minute you open the lid, air rushes in, as nature abhors a vacuum. The pressure inside the container is soon the same as that outside. And so it is with the earth's energy rushing into your body as soon as it gets an opportunity. Whilst that opportunity occurs most easily when in contact with the earth, it can also be learnt, even when not in contact with the ground, using visualisation techniques.

Christopher McDougall's "Born to Run"[87] investigates how we were born to run without hi-tech shoes and without injury.

When humans travel into space, they just float because of a lack of gravity. They take travel sickness medication to help the inner ear, which is responsible for balance, to respond correctly[88]. This medication has been found to help with SpLDs too; in reality all that is needed is simply to learn to ground yourself and enjoy the experience.

What is wrong with giving parents hope of a positive outcome? If they don't have hope, they are unlikely to succeed; a negative outlook can be self-fulfilling. We know miracles happen every day.

New Perspectives Books and CDs

New Perspectives has brought together a unique set of books and CDs, for those wishing to explore how they can become the person they want to be. The objective is to offer you the tools with which to start your own personal developmental journey around specific areas on which you're focused, such as:

- Improving general health.
- Recovery from illness.
- Overcoming learning difficulties.
- Moving on from long standing health problems.
- Building confidence.
- Reducing stress, releasing what is no longer important.
- Improving family and business relationships.
- Better communications between yourself and others.
- Well-being for women.
- Recover from physical injury.
- Eliminating food intolerances.

If you find a particular book or CD of value for an immediate need in your life, you may become curious to understand more about other aspects. We would encourage you to move to other areas that you may feel appropriate.

The books have many stories, examples, client experiences, pictures, dialogue and sometime workbook pages to fully illustrate the point and help you move forward. They will be challenging. Personal change can only be achieved with commitment. Several books employ the healing power of stories that have passed down through the centuries.

As individuals grow within themselves, they find:

- Some of the daily worries of modern living melt away.
- Focus changes to things that are really important.
- A calmer more grounded individual is less affected by negative experience and far more able to cope with challenges.
- Long term illnesses change and start to shift.
- Energy and fun increase hugely.
- Inner wisdom shines through.

All of the New Perspectives books are designed for "the man/woman in the street"; they work because they just make sense.

References

[1] Art Giser, is the creator of Energetic NLP, www.energeticnlp.com

[2] Hickmott, Olive and Bendefy, Andrew, Seeing Spells Achieving, MX Publishing, 2006

[3] Arthur Conan Doyle, Sr, creator of the detective Sherlock Holmes

[4] The Early Years Foundation Stage was published in 2008, by the Department for Children, Schools and Families. ISBN: 978-1-84775-128-7

[5] I and many of my clients have let go of the spelling and reading challenges of Dyslexia, while retaining the other great attributes of being able to see things from different perspectives etc. One lady I met, managed to overcome her reading problem by relaxing on an aeroplane, reading Harry Potter. This is text written in a very creative way which triggers the occipito-temporal region of the brain – the area needed for visualising words. In her relaxed state, visual spelling and reading simply flowed. My own measure of success is that I never read a book for pleasure until reading to my baby son. With his help I managed to read aloud for the first time and then, when I found visual spelling, my ability to read books dramatically increased. Now I can read a reasonable book in a day and can remember it. You will find more stories at www.empoweringlearning.co.uk

[6] Dr. Cheri Florance has documented many case studies, including that of her own son, who "had many labels including ADD; Autism; mental retardation; learning disabled; multiple-handicapped; deafness and PDD (Pervasive Developmental Disorder). The real problem, as I was to discover, was his over-working visual brain was interfering with the development of his auditory-verbal brain, imitating the symptoms of many of the above disorders. My career as a brain scientist before my son's birth guided me towards this discovery. My subsequent life's work has been devoted to

helping other highly visual children and adults to like-wise become symptoms free." She has called these highly visual children "Mavericks".

[7] The Open University definition

[8]Many students with SpLD, suffer from a visual-perceptual discomfort and disturbance which is sometimes known as Meares-Irlen Syndrome. This affects their reading of print on white paper, on overheads and slides, and use of a computer. www.irlen.com

[9] Comorbidity describes these overlaps. There is considerable information about comorbidity and here are just a couple of the extracts. According to an article published on Medscape, one study of children with Asperger's Syndrome showed that 62.5% of the participants also showed clinical symptoms indicating attention-deficit hyperactivity disorder (ADHD). Dr. Genel in *Attention Magazine* said that research studies showed that as much as 65% of children with ADHD will have one or more comorbid condition at some point in their lives. Dr. Genel's review of follow-up studies of children with ADHD and studies of adults who were later diagnosed with ADHD indicated that the disorder often persists into adulthood. Common conditions that often co-exist with ADHD are Dyslexia and Asperger's.

[10] Florance, Dr. Cheri, *A boy beyond reach*, Simon & Schuster, 2004

[11] Bernadette McClean, Principal, Helen Arkell Centre, www.arkellcentre.org.uk

[12] West, Thomas G, *In the mind's eye*, Prometheur books, 1943, P29

[13] Stephen Wiltshire: The human camera
http://www.youtube.com/watch?v=a8YXZTlwTAU

[14] Sir Ken Robinson, The Changing Educational Paradigms,
http://www.youtube.com/watch?v=zDZFcDGpL4U

[15] The Little Boy, by Helen E. Buckley, http://craiglien.com/thelittleboy.htm printed in Jack Canfield's Chicken Soup

[16] International Teaching Seminars, NLP Practitioner training, www.itsnlp.com, Ian McDermott

[17] Art Giser's Energetic NLP training incorporates training on self concept and self esteem, www.energeticnlp.com

[18] International Teaching Seminars, NLP Practitioner training, www.itsnlp.com, Ian McDermott

[19] Rizzolatti, Giscomo, and Fogassi, Leonardo, and Gallese, Vittorio, Mirrors in the Mind. Scientific American, Nov 2006, Neuroscience section Ramachandran, Vilayanur S. and Oberman, Lindsay M. Broken Mirrors, A theory of Autism. Scientific American Reports 2007

[20] Sir Ken Robinson, The Changing Educational Paradigms, http://www.youtube.com/watch?v=zDZFcDGpL4U

[21] Richard Bandler, www.richardbandler.com

[22] Hickmott, Olive, Recover Your Energy, MX Publishing, 2009. Valuable resource for Chronic Fatigue, ME and any form of exhaustion.

[23] Hickmott, Olive and Knighton, Sarah, You too can do health, MX Publishing, 2007

[24] Mctaggart, Lynne, The Field: The Quest for the Secret Force of the Universe, Element; New Ed edition (7 April 2003)

[25] Art Giser, is the creator of Energetic NLP, www.energeticnlp.com

[26] CDs of the meditations can be purchased from www.bridgestosuccess.co.uk. There is also a complete talking book available for this book, to assist those who struggle with reading.

[27] We are taking a very NLP perspective that this is just a model, a way to work with your mind, body and spirit, to explore the effects when working with this model.

[28] Weebles is a trademark for several lines of children's roly-poly toys originating in Hasbro's Playskool division on July 23, 1971. Shaped like eggs with a weight at the fat, or bottom end, they wobble when pushed, but never fall completely over.

[29] John Friedlander, www.psychicdevelopment.cc

[30] This area is known as your hara in Eastern traditions

[31] Fran Stockley, Natural Health and Energy Coach, www.franstockley.com

[32] Childre, Doc and Martin, Howard, *The Heartmath Solution*, The Institute of Heartmath's revolutionary programme for engaging the power of the Heart's Intelligence. http://www.heartmath.org/

[33] Proprioception — from Latin *proprius*, meaning "one's own," and *perception* — is one of the human senses. There are between nine and 21 in all, depending on which sense researcher you ask. Rather than sensing external reality, proprioception is the sense of the orientation of one's limbs in space. Learning any new motor skill involves training our proprioceptive sense. Anything that involves moving our arms or legs in a precise way without looking at them invokes it.

[34] Dame Evelyn Glennie's official web-site www.evelyn.co.uk

[35] Shaywitz, Sally, Overcoming Dyslexia, Vintage, 2005, P79 . Dr. Sally E. Shaywitz is a professor of Learning Development at Yale University.

[36] Robertson, Ian. *The Mind's Eye*, Bantam Book, 2002

[37] Current research in NLP, volume 1 – Proceedings of the 2008 conference, edited by Paul Tosey. *A critical review of past research into the neuro-logical programming of eye-accessing cues model*, Diamantopoulos, Georgios, Wolley, Sandra, Span, Michael

[38] The National Autistic Society reports the frequent occurrence of one parent managing to cope with and accept a child as being autistic, whilst the other one can't. We can only guess at the correlation with a parent's symptoms.

[39] Bruce Lipton's research on DNA. http://www.brucelipton.com/

[40] As a Director of the International Association for Health and Learning (IHL) I believe in just that, collaboration and empowering people to achieve for themselves. Take a look at www.tiahl.org

[41] Empowering Learning is the name of Olive Hickmott's business, www.empoweringlearning.co.uk

[42] Dr Cheri Florance, President, Brain Engineering Laboratories, www.cheriflorance.com

[43] You Tube on Validation: http://www.youtube.com/watch?v=Cbk980jV7Ao

[44] The strategy has been researched by Tom Malloy at the University of Utah and F. Loiselle at the University of Moncton in New Brunswick, Canada 1985. Both research projects showed a significant change in people's ability to spell accurately after learning the NLP Spelling Strategy. These studies support the NLP Spelling Strategy specifically and the NLP notion of Eye Accessing Cues and Sensory Representation System strategies in general. They are reported in: Dilts, R. and Epstein, T., *Dynamic Learning*, Meta, Capitola, California,1995, and elsewhere in many NLP books. The NLP University Press, www.nlpuniversitypress.com, Spelling Strategy P1285-1290, Research P1109 Malloy, Thomas E. Principles of teaching Cognitive Strategies, Dept of Psychology, University of Utah, 2007

[45] "With Phonetic Reading you read by translating what you see into a sound and that sound gives you your meaning. It does though mean that your speed is limited to how fast you can 'hear' the words. That is about 350 – 400 words per minute. When reading by visualising you see the word and your recognition memory gives you your understanding. Here your speed is limited to how fast you can see the words and that is about 2,000 – 3,000 words per minute. We call this Accelerated Reading. With Quantum Reading™ you read through peripheral vision and, with a book, you take in both pages at the same time. Now your speed is limited to how fast you turn the pages or about 20,000 to 30,000 words per minute. To advance from phonetic reading requires a change in skill set, but more importantly a change in your beliefs about reading"
http://www.thethinkingconsultancy.com/ the home of Quantum reading™

If you are in the USA, Gerry Hughes will be a valuable source of information at the The Neuro-Linguistic Learning Center, Eldorado Hills, California. He specialises in helping children, teens and adults overcome a variety of learning challenges. He offers 'one-stop-shopping' approach to educational and behavioral programs providing parents with all the tools they need to help their child and family succeed.
www.swish4fish.com/

[46] This is one of the areas that the IHL plans to research.

[47] Dyslexia Research Trust, http://www.dyslexic.org.uk/research-visual.html

[48] Shaywitz, Sally, *Overcoming Dyslexia*, Random House USA Inc; 2005, p79
Dr. Sally E. Shaywitz is a professor of Pediatric Neurology at Yale University

[49] Those who have bought this book can download a workbook from www.bridgestosuccess.co.uk free of charge.

[50] High frequency words are included in the UK's National Literacy Strategy. These lists are used worldwide for teaching English in primary school. English as a Second Language seems to focus more on nouns first.

[51] You can register to download a workbook from www.bridgestosuccess.co.uk

[52] Dennison, Paul E. and Gail E., *Brain Gym*, Edu-Kinesthetics Inc, 1992

[53] A recipe stand may help - try www.bookchair.com

[54] The King's Speech - the Oscar winning film. The story of King George VI's ascension to the throne and the speech therapist who helped the King. -Also see original film footage of King George VI

[55] The Neuro-logical levels are a useful model to help you understand your experience.

[56] Jen Tiller's page on good breathing http://www.jentiller.com/page6.htm

[57] www.mindfulness.com

[58] Kris Hallbom and Tim Hallbom, Dynamic Spin release, http://www.dynamicspinrelease.com/

[59] The Helen Arkell Teaching Clocks, www.arkellcentre.org.uk

[60] Quantum learning, Dominic O'Brien, Nightingale Conant. http://www.nightingaleconant.co.uk/prod_detail.aspx?product=Quantum_Memory_Power&dloc=2

[61] Buzan, Tony, *Mind Maps for Kids*, London, Thorsons, 2003

[62] University of Bedfordshire, Herbert Daly, research project http://www.beds.ac.uk/news/2011/mar/110316-visual

[63] Picoult, Jodi, *House Rules*, Hodder Paperbacks, 2010

[64] Picoult, Jodi, *House Rules*, Hodder Paperbacks, 2010

[65] Rev. Audrey, W, *Thomas the Tank Engine*, Egmont Books

[66] Rizzolatti, Giscomo, and Fogassi, Leonardo, and Gallese, Vittorio, *Mirrors in the Mind*. Scientific American, Nov 2006, Neuroscience section Ramachandran, Vilayanur S. and Oberman, Lindsay M. *Broken Mirrors, A theory of Autism*. Scientific American Reports 2007

[67] Picoult, Jodi, *House Rules*, Hodder Paperbacks, 2010

[68] Tricking (short for "martial arts tricking") is the informal name of a relatively new underground alternative sport movement, combining martial arts, gymnastics, and other activities to create an "aesthetic blend of flips, kicks, and twists."

[69] Rowling, J. K, Harry Potter series of books, Bloomsbury Publishing PLC; 1st edition (8 Oct 2001)

[70] Down Syndrome Educational International. Sue Buckley, www.dseinternational.org

[71] From Holt, John, How children Learn, Harmondsworth, England, Penguin Books, 1970

[72] Picoult, Jodi, *House Rules*, Hodder Paperbacks, 2010

[73] Gardner, Nuala A Friend Like Henry ,Hodder Paperbacks ,2008

[74] Down Syndrome Educational International. Sue Buckley, www.dseinternational.org

[75] Holt, John, How children Learn, Harmondsworth, England, Penguin Books, 1970

[76] Government Green paper consultation. Support and aspiration: A new approach to special educational needs and disability. Presented to Parliament by the Secretary of State for Education, March 2011

[77] Quote from the Government Green Paper, see (76) above

[78] SEN Magazine, Issue 52, May-June 2011, Andy Burnham, Shaw Secretary of State for Education, P24

[79] SEN Magazine, Issue 52, May-June 2011, Neville Broan, Principle of Maple Hayes Dyslexia School and Research centre,, P29

[80] House of Commons, Education Committee - First Report, 26th January 2011

[81] The Early Years Foundation Stage was published in 2008, by the Department for Children, Schools and Families. ISBN: 978-1-84775-128-7

[82] SEN Magazine, Issue 52, May-June 2011, Baroness Warlock, Chaired the Committee of Inquiry into the education of handicapped children and Young People that produced the Warnock Report (1978), P26

[83] Ober, Clint and Sinatra, Stephen and Zucker, Martin, *Earthing: The most important health discovery ever?* Basic Health Publications, 2010

[84] According to the late Dr William Rossi, a Massachusetts podiatrist and footwear industry historian. Footware News, 1997. Author of 8 books and over 400 articles.

[85] Wolfe, David, www.davidworlfe.com

[86] University of Illinois at Urbana-Champaign, Landscape and human health Laboratory. www. http://lhhl.illinois.edu/adhd.htm. The information here is from the original scientific articles:

- Faber Taylor, A., Kuo, F.E., & Sullivan, W.C. (2001). "Coping with ADD: The surprising connection to green play settings." *Environment and Behavior*, 33(1), 54-77.
- Kuo, F.E., & Faber Taylor, A. (2004). "A potential natural treatment for Attention-Deficit/Hyperactivity Disorder: Evidence from a national study." *American Journal of Public Health*, 94(9), 1580-1586.
- Faber Taylor, A. & Kuo, F.E. (2009). "Children with attention deficits concentrate better after walk in the park." *Journal of Attention Disorders*, 12, 402-409.

[87] McDougall, Christopher, *Born to Run: A Hidden Tribe, Superathletes, and the Greatest Race the World Has Never Seen*.

[88] Dr Levinson has spent the past 30 years devising the theory that Dyslexia is connected more with the inner ears and cerebellum, which controls balance and co-ordination. He uses the travels sickness pills taken by astronauts to help clients.

Lightning Source UK Ltd.
Milton Keynes UK
UKOW031221311011

181226UK00001B/91/P